The Complete Encyclopedia of

Practical Palmistry

The
Complete Encyclopedia
of Practical

Palmistry

Marcel Broekman

PRENTICE-HALL, INC.
Englewood Cliffs, N.J.

The Complete Encyclopedia of Practical Palmistry by Marcel Broekman

Copyright © 1972 by Marcel Broekman

Printed in the United States of America

Prentice-Hall International, Inc., London
Prentice-Hall of Australia, Pty. Ltd., North Sydney
Prentice-Hall of Canada, Ltd., Toronto
Prentice-Hall of India Private Ltd., New Delhi
Prentice-Hall of Japan, Inc., Tokyo

To Minnie

CONTENTS

PART THREE—ANALYSIS

Advice to the reader
Abnormal mentality
Achievement
Compatibility
Energy
Future events
Happiness
Health
Homosexuality
Logic
Love
Negative markings
Occupations
Success
Wisdom

PART FOUR

Sample readings

Palmistry
as a Basic Philosophy

For many centuries, theories were presented as to the meaning of the various lines on the hand, but no one could logically explain the existence of these lines. They are *not* merely folds or creases; more than a few lines in any palm tend to go "against the grain." Their cause is unknown. But they speak very clearly, in a complex language.

The various theories culminated in the works of Count Louis Hamon, better known as Cheiro, who became extremely well-known due to the accuracy of his predictions. Unfortunately, he also claimed Occult powers, so that it has become difficult to separate the technical (*reading*) aspect of palmistry from the psychic (*Occult*) portion of his readings which resulted in those brilliant predictions.

In my study of the hands of many people in all walks of life, it has become very apparent that past events leave easily detected deformations or markings in the major lines of the hand. (If the foot were as easily accessible for interpretation of lines as the hand is, there would be no objection in principle against reading foot lines.)

My own work has been chiefly concerned with the purely topographical aspect of the hand lines. I hope that the mere act of organizing these lines will result in ascribing a proper meaning to each. I do not know if all lines will lend themselves to this type of interpretation, however. There are also some lines in the hand which have been described in so many diverse manners by well-accepted palmists that I will not deal with them in the course of this book.

Since I have no interest in the occult or in telling the future —although that is possible—I am not offering any thoughts as to why or how the lines indicate what they do. It is evident, however, that the information contained in these markings is of immense importance to the person in whose hands these marks appear.

Palmistry can be used as a common-sense everyday guide for living. Our hands seem to reflect our inner self, telling us our strengths and weaknesses.

I believe we cannot understand more of life and ourselves

than the hand lines show us to be capable of. Each and every one of us has a limit for knowledge—some higher, some lower. But palmistry can take us along our road in this world and guide us toward the maximum goal we are able to reach. It will tell us when we are underachieving and when we are doing our best. Although it does not steer us day by day or month by month, it tells us what we may expect over a period of a few years.

If our hand is a hand we consider beneath our capacity, we have a choice to improve it. And the interesting feature is that our hand prints will tell us if we are improving or getting worse. Since the lines do change to a certain extent, I usually make reference prints of the lines for later comparison to determine the trend and extent of change.

Of course, such knowledge has always been a double-edged sword. I only appreciate knowledge that helps people. I would never say anything to a subject that would be of negative value. I would even be cautious to impart too much self-knowledge; too much thought and inner searching may drive a weak mind over the brink. It might stop the person from functioning, and our aim on this planet seems to be to function and become relatively happy with our lot.

Knowledge is also a potent help to the person who wants to see progress. And here we find a great help in our hand lines. Do these mean the same thing every time? Can we find simple clues to genetic factors? Can we change the lines by our will in every case? What in ourselves corresponds to our hand lines? Do the stars or the universe influence our will, our hand lines and our future? What is that time factor which is so clearly seen in our hands?

Today the search has become simpler because computers can help us with correspondences. By coding the lines and the events ascribed to them, it has become possible to analyze their meaning on a large scale. The investigation at present should be limited to past *events* and their impressions, genetic correspondence in sensitivity to illnesses, and mental disorders. Our efforts in all of these cases should be to find out if all those whose hands show similar markings also show similarities in character and experience. In my investigation of hundreds of hands, the correspondence has always been there, but to make a rule definite (if not always explicable), the correspondence should be one hundred percent. And when the answers start to come in, we will have opened a new path for scientific investigation.

In the many works on palmistry which I have read I have always felt a great lack of organization. Living in the age of the computer as we do, we like to see facts presented to us in a simple, easy to understand manner. With the lines in the hand, which are the main concern of my study, I have found no book that covers their position in the palm in a manner that I would consider topographical. I have worked out a way in which I can quickly describe and locate a given line with its generally accepted meaning, and it is this catalogue of lines that forms the basis for this book, written to make it easy for the reader to find the meaning of any particular mark or line and to enable the student of topographical palmistry to catalogue lines for analysis.

The questions most often posed to the reader of hands are: "What does this line mean?" and "What can you tell me about. . . ?" Therefore, although I have named the various regions of the hand according to old custom, I have separated all aspects of the hand into two categories: event marks and character marks. All lines and markings dealing with *events* are treated separately in Part One of the book, listed with numbers below 100. The exact meaning of any event mark appearing separately in the hand will be explained in the first part. The description of the mark includes information as to which other markings modify this mark—and to what extent.

Since past events show clearly in the hand lines, it might be surmised that future events foretell themselves in the same manner. Before attempting to interpret any event marks, however, it is of the greatest importance to have a clear understanding of the interrelation of the major lines throughout the hand.

Part Two deals with lines as indications of character and potential, listed with numbers above 100. The character marks also indicate the *nature* of illnesses and any physical or mental shortcoming a person may have; if an event mark shows the occurrence of an illness, then the character mark will indicate the nature. Character lines, together with other markings in the hand, give a good indication of the character and potential of people. They can help the subject develop most wanted traits and suppress those that are a hindrance rather than an asset. This book, therefore, will also be of great help to guidance counselors who may not want to study topographical palmistry but are interested in the positive aid such knowledge will give them. In this section I have used only descriptions I have personally confirmed.

Part Three deals with topics—health, wealth, love and so forth—and what special combinations to look for in each case. The answer to the question "What can you tell me about . . . ?" can be given by either an event line or a character marking. We must remember that all *events* are contained in lines, whereas the character traits will be seen in a few simple specifics of the hand and also in *the character lines,* which differ from the event lines. Since no one can encounter all of the many possible combinations of lines in the hand, from time to time I have used the interpretations of other line readers as to the meaning of a certain combination. The "live" hand often does not show detail that appears in a print. Moreover, prints can be more easily referred to during the course of the analysis, and can of course be saved for future reference.

To make a print of the hand lines, the following materials are needed:

* One tube of fingerprint ink (available from Faurot, Inc., 299 Broadway, New York, N.Y. 10007, among others).

* A smooth surface, such as glass or metal, on which to roll out the ink.

* One hard rubber roller, as sold by photographic supply stores.

* Glossy paper.

[16]

Squeeze a little ink on the smooth surface and roll the roller through the ink, coating it evenly with the ink. Apply the roller to the hand to be printed. Place the glossy paper on a surface that is not too firm, like a rubber mat, and carefully apply the hand to the paper. Roll the hand off the paper toward the edge of the hand so the percussion is printed also. Carefully lift the hand off the paper.

The ink is easily removed with any commercial hand cleaner such as Quikee or Gre-Solvent. If an outline of the fingers is wanted, draw in the outlines before lifting off the hand. Disposa-pad material commonly used for making footprints of newborn infants, together with special paper and instructions, is also available from Faurot, Inc. I blot the entire palm with the Disposa-pad *after outlining the fingers* on the sensitive paper.

Part 1

Event Markings

PROCEDURE FOR ANALYSIS

Determine the Major Hand of a subject
The hand that shows the active life of the subject, and therefore the hand used in determining events and active character traits, is called the Major Hand. The hand used to determine inherited factors is called the Minor Hand.

The *Major Hand* of a subject is the *right hand* for *right-handed people,* the *left hand* for *left-handed people.*

The *Minor Hand* of a subject is the other hand: the *left hand* for *right-handed people,* the *right hand* for *left-handed people.*

The next step is to recognize the lines.

The charts in this book have been prepared to make it easier to locate and identify lines referred to in the text. The left hand (Minor Hand) is illustrated in each case. *Read actual events in the Major Hand only.*

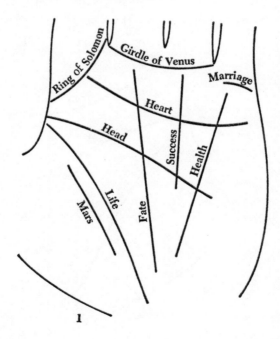

1

On the first illustration, the six major lines—Life, Head, Heart, Fate, Sun (Success) and Health—have been drawn in. Their position here and on the following charts denotes where they may generally be found in the average hand.

Find these six major lines in the hand under observation so that they will not be confused with one of the secondary lines (see section 55). There are some hands which do not have all of the Major Lines. *Missing Lines* are listed in the section dealing with those lines.

The hand-line analyst who examines the hands or handprints for past, present or future will save much trouble by remembering certain general rules:

* When the Life Line and the Head Line are clearly and sharply marked, without breaks, we can expect that health will not be a problem for the subject.
* Temporary illnesses can still be seen as functions of the

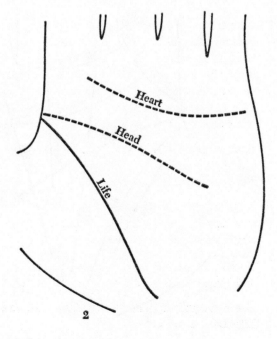

2

Health Line, but the overall prognosis is one of good general health.

* When these same lines are ill-defined, chained, or wavy and interrupted, the opposite will be found to be true. When lines are doubled, they are reinforced; when tasseled at the end, they are weakened in later life.

Details for each line will be discussed under the particular heading.

2

The Life Line

All major events are marked on the Life Line. The Life Line starts at the side of the hand and progresses down toward the wrist.

Lines that may be confused with the Life Line

The Mars Line .... see section 119 F 1
Influence Lines .... see section 18 B
A portion of the Fate Line .... see section 29 A

Like all major lines, the Life Line may exhibit certain characteristics that differ for each subject. It may appear as a straight unbroken line, it may show a chained character or it may have islands marked along its length. There will often be seen lines crossing it in various directions. Sometimes the Life Line shows breaks in one or both hands or dots. Combinations of the above can often be found in many hands.

Each of these marks and markings have a special meaning, but in the case of the Life Line, the marks directly affect the *physical* world of the subject.

Some hands will be completely covered with fine lines. Before proceeding to analyze these hands, read section 12, which describes the nervous hand.

3

To find the *age* on the Life Line, use gauge A for large hands and gauge B for medium and small hands.

Use a magnifying glass to determine the exact nature of the Life Line at all ages.

[23]

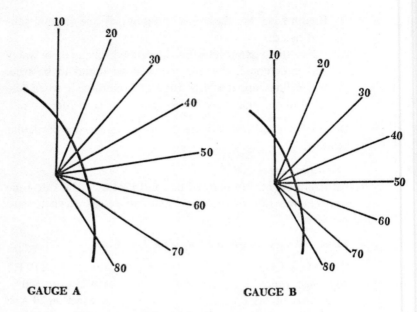

GAUGE A   **GAUGE B**

Note on age determination

The Heart Line, the Fate and Sun Lines as well as the Health Line also have inherent age markings—which are discussed under their various headings. There is sometimes a small variation in interpretation by other analysts. Cheiro in his interpretation of the starting point of the Health Line reads it as I do, starting from the Little Finger downwards. Psychos and Desbarolles assume the starting point to be on Luna and read this line up toward the Little Finger. All agree to the meaning of the quality of the Line, but the discussion arises when the period is considered. To avoid the problem I consult the Life Line, which will invariably note any serious physical disability together with its time span. (This seems to confirm my method of reading from the Mount of Mercury downwards.)

---

4   The *straight and unbroken* Life Line indicates a normal life. Events are marked on the Life Line as follows:
Lines sweeping up from the Life Line—see section 10.

Lines sweeping down from the Life Line—see section 11.

Lines smoothly crossing the Life Line—see section 12.

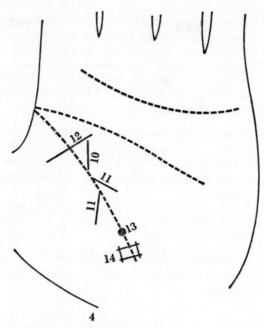

4

Dots in the Life Line—see section 13.

Squares on the Life Line—see section 14.

5   *The chained Life Line* is the symptom of a health problem. The health problem involved is described in sections 39 through 42; also Part Two, section 126. Events on the chained Life Line are the same as marked in section 15.

6   *The Life Line with islands* indicates acute sickness or injury, described in section 16.

7   *The Life Line with breaks* indicates grave danger, accidents or death. If the break appears in the Major Hand only, see section 17.

8   *If the break in the Life Line* appears in the Minor Hand only, see section 17 A. If the break appears in both hands, see section 17 C.

9   *Event markings* for all forms of Life Line are the same as in section 4.

10   *Lines sweeping up from the Life Line:* The general rule for
lines that sweep up from the Life Line is the same as for
most lines that run from the wrist to the fingers: They indicate success and achievements in varying degree.

Using the age gauge, first determine the age at which the line
sweeps up from the Life Line. Now determine the *direction*
and *ending* of the upswept lines.

10 A   *The Line sweeps up in the direction of the Index Finger* (Jupiter): At the age indicated on the Life Line, the subject
achieves success in a personal ambition. In the younger
years it means scholastic distinction; in later years, business
achievement.

The ending of the upswept line, in the direction of Jupiter,
may be:

10 A 1   *Ending quite close to the Life Line* (not reaching other major
lines): These short lines to Jupiter indicate minor achievements.

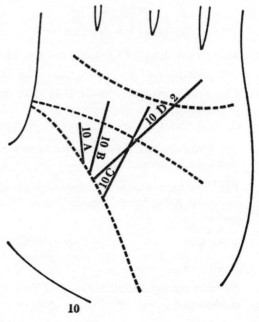

10

10 A 2 *Ending far up from the Life Line* (cutting through the hand far into the region under the Index Finger): Indicates much farther-reaching ambitions which are achieved.

10 B *The line sweeps up in the direction of the Middle Finger* (Saturn): At the age indicated on the Life Line, the subject achieves wealth through personal efforts.

The *ending* of the upswept line, in the direction of Saturn, may be:

10 B 1 *Ending quite close to the Life Line:* This short line indicates a minor achievement.

10 B 2 *Ending far up along the Fate Line* (see section 27): Indicates a major achievement.

10 C *The line sweeps up in the direction of the Ring Finger* (Apollo): At the age indicated on the Life Line, the subject achieves creative success.

The *ending* of the upswept line, in the direction of Apollo, may be:

10 C 1 *Ending quite close to the Life Line:* Indicates a minor achievement in the arts.

10 C 2 *Ending far up from the Life Line and crossing the Fate Line:* Indicates a major achievement in the arts.

10 C 3 *Ending in the area under the Ring Finger* after sweeping from the Life Line and crossing the Fate Line: This is the sign of the most accomplished and creative artists.

10 D *The Line sweeps up in the direction of the Little Finger* (Mercury): At the age indicated on the Life Line, the subject achieves success in science or business.

Do not confuse this line with the Health Line (section 39).

The ending of the upswept line, in the direction of Mercury, may be:

10 D 1 *Ending quite close to the Life Line:* Indicates a minor achievement.

10 D 2 *Ending under the little finger:* Indicates great success in business and science. This line is also known as the Health Line (section 39) and denotes a special type person described under Mercury, section 110 D.

11   *Lines sweeping down from the Life Line:* The general rule for lines sweeping downward from a major line is that they indicate negative trends. In the case of the Life Line, all lines sweeping down are obstructions. Using the age gauge, first determine the age at which the line sweeps down from the Life Line. Now determine the *direction* and *ending* of the downswept lines.

11 A   *Small hairlines sweeping down* from the Life Line, clinging close to the Life Line: These indicate physical weakness at the age indicated.

11 B   *Small hairlines sweeping down* at the end of the Life Line: These indicate gradual physical weakening at the end of life.

11 C   *A heavy line sweeping down* from the Life Line at the cen-

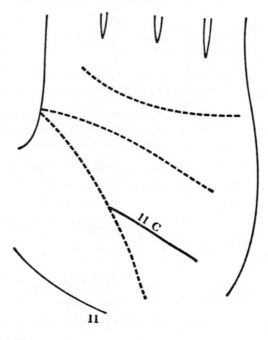

ter of the hand, like a branch of the Life Line, and ending on or near Luna: This indicates a great desire for change.

11 C 1 *The type of change* in a hard hand, firm to the touch and with a long first phalanx of the Thumb, indicates extensive travel.

11 C 2 *The type of change* in a soft, flabby hand is found in escapism, by the use of any undesirable means, detrimental to the individual and people connected with him or her.

12 *Lines smoothly crossing the Life Line*

A great number of fine lines crossing the Life Line at all ages: This is usually seen on a hand completely covered with fine lines. It indicates a very sensitive subject, highly nervous and high-strung. Do not try to interpret these fine lines as individual event marks. The event markings will be much longer and deeper than these small fine lines.

Using the age gauge, first determine the age at which the line

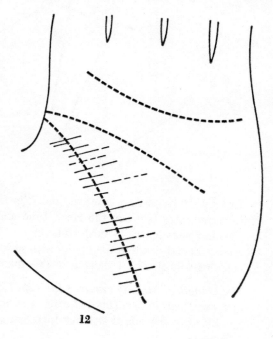

12

crosses the Life Line. Now determine the *direction* and *ending* of the crossing line.

12 A *The smoothly crossing line cuts only the Life Line* and ends before cutting any other lines: This indicates interference by relatives in the subject's personal life.

12 B *The smoothly crossing line cuts the Life Line and the Fate Line:* This indicates interference in business and work.

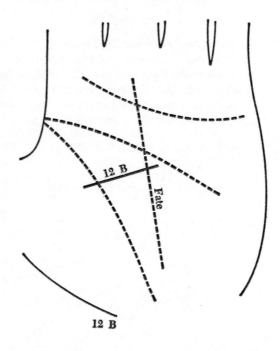

12 B

12 C *The smoothly crossing line cuts the Life Line and the Head Line* and ends between the Head Line and the Heart Line: This indicates a serious misfortune caused by close relations. An accidental death in the family with serious financial repercussions will also be indicated in this manner.

12 D *The smoothly crossing line cuts the Life Line, the Head Line and the Heart Line:* This indicates a serious misfortune experienced in the affections: lost love, for example.

[30]

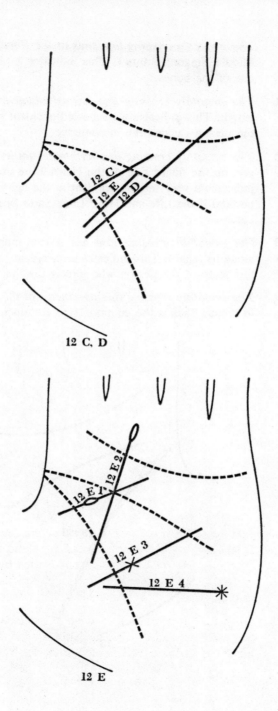

12 C, D

12 E

12 E   *The smoothly crossing line ends at the Head Line* under the Middle Finger (Saturn): This indicates a physical break in one of the bones.

12 E 1   *The smoothly crossing line has an island* marked along its length: This indicates a connected accident or misfortune to the person causing the interference.

12 E 2   *The smoothly crossing line terminates under the middle finger,* on the finger side of the Heart Line in an *island:* This indicates a very serious accident at the age indicated. It will be fatal if the Life and Head Lines show breaks at the same age.

12 E 3   *The smoothly crossing line has a star* marked somewhere along its length: This indicates an accident to and sometimes the death of the person who affects the life.

12 E 4   *The smoothly crossing line terminates at the Mount of Luna in a star:* This is the common sign for suicide.

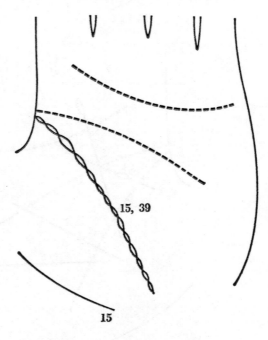

15, 39

15

13   *Dots marked on the Life Line* are indications of temporary illness. Identify the age and type of illness connected with the spot. Read only illness marks in the Major Hand (see section 1). Determine the type of illness by using section 50. See also Part Two, section 126, for "Illnesses according to type."

14   *Squares* are preservation marks not often seen on the smooth Life Line since they usually preserve a broken Life Line (see illustration, section 17 B 2).

15   *The chained Life Line* is the sign of poor health. If the chain formation is seen only in the Minor Hand (described in section 1) this is merely an inherited trait indicating that one or both parents were in poor health.

If the chain formation is seen in the Major Hand also, the subject is affected. The *form* in which the poor health presents itself is described in section 50 and under Part Two, section 126, "Illnesses according to type."

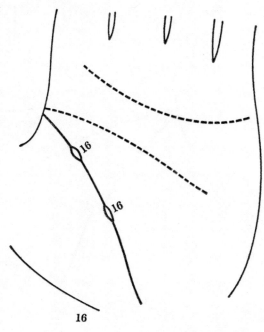

Event markings are the same as for the unbroken Life Line (sections 10 through 14).

16   *The Life Line with islands:* This marking denotes an illness for the time indicated by the length of the island. To determine the nature of the illness, see sections 39 through 42 and section 50. Also consult Part Two, section 126, for "Illnesses according to type."

17   *The Life Line with breaks:* This is a bad sign. If the break occurs in the Minor Hand only, it indicates a serious illness or accident. But a break in both hands indicates death. A break in the Major Hand only means a severe accident, not an illness.

First determine the age at which the break occurs.

17 A   *Only the Minor Hand has a break:* If this occurred in the past, check for *repair lines*. The repair lines are lines running very close and parallel to the Life Line. This means that the

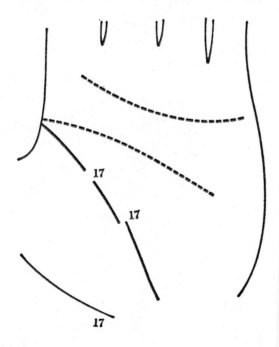

Life was in acute danger but was preserved by the individual's own actions.

A square (which consists of two connecting sets of parallel lines) over the break serves the same purpose. The danger was man-made, not caused by illness.

17 B *Only the Major Hand has a break:* The break in the Life Line indicates a danger. Since the Minor Hand does not have a break, it is not a fatal occurrence.

Check for the following repair lines:

17 B 1 *A sister line or Mars Line* closely following the Life Line repairs the break.

17 B 2 A *square* over the break repairs the break.

17 B 3 An *overlap* (closely joined) indicates a very great change, usually of location, deeply affecting the individual.

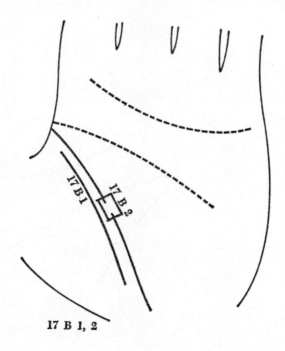

17 B 1, 2

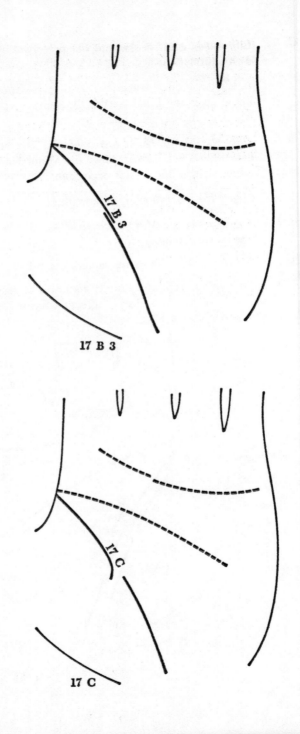

17 B 3

17 C

17 C *Both hands show a break in the Life Line:* This is the most severe form of break. Repair markings are found as above. The general rule is that the wider the break, the more severe the case, especially if the upper break hooks back into the thumb area (Venus). The nature of the incident is found by first checking the entire hand for illnesses on other lines (sections 23 and 24, 39 through 42 and 50). If no illnesses are indicated, it must be assumed that an accident will occur at the age indicated.

18 *Life Line with miscellaneous marks:* A combination of unbroken, chained and laddered Life Line is often encountered. These are read by age periods. In the Major Hand, a Life Line that shows chaining at the beginning and becomes straight indicates childhood illnesses and good health later.

18 A *The ladder formation on the Life Line* means the same as the chained Life Line (section 15) and is read the same way.

18 B *Influence Lines following parallel to the Life Line:* Close to

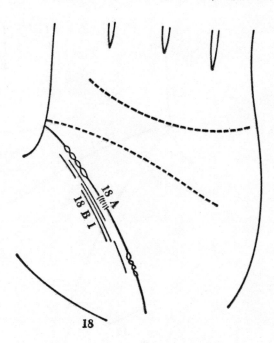

the Life Line, they indicate the influence of other people. They indicate by their approaching or receding from the Life Line whether the influence will become stronger or will lessen. These lines are as important as the Affection Line (section 43) in determining personal attachments. They differ from repair lines (section 17 B 1) in that they do recede from or approach the Life Line.

18 B 1 *A great number of close parallel lines to the Life Line* indicate a person very much under the influence of others. The age period is read on the Life Line.

19 *The Head Line:* The Head Line starts at the Thumb side of the hand and progresses across the hand to the percussion or slopes somewhat toward the wrist.

Lines that may be confused with the Head Line

The Heart Line . . . . section 26

A portion of the Sun Line . . . . section 38

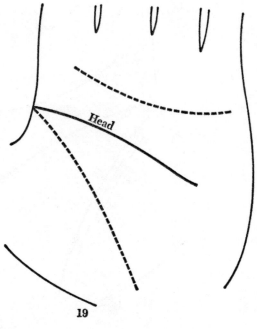

19

20   *Examining the Head Line:* Like the Life Line, the Head Line is one of the major lines in the hand. It will show many variations: It may be smooth and unbroken, chained or marked with islands, broken in one or both hands. Each of these variations is an indication of a characteristic of the individual, while some are signs of physical occurrences past, present and future.

21   *The smooth, unbroken Head Line:* This is the normal Head Line to look for. Since this line mainly deals with character, most variations are listed in Part Two, section 114. The absence of breaks, dots and islands indicates good physical and mental health, without accidents—unless illnesses are marked on the Life Line (sections 13, 15, 16, 17 and 18).

22   *The chained Head Line:* This is a character marking. See section 114 G 2.

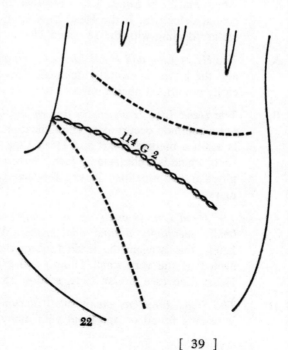

23   *The Head Line with islands:* This indicates danger to the brain, in the form of a physical blow, or brain disease. This mark is also often found together with a strong line crossing the Life Line, indicating the age at which the occurrence takes place. Broken bones are marked by an island in the Head Line, under the middle finger (Saturn), and a strong crossing line in the Life Line. When islands are noted on the Head Line, it is imperative to examine the Life Line for additional clues.

24   *The Head Line with breaks:* This is a sign of serious trouble. If the break occurs in both hands under the middle finger, it usually indicates an early death. Repair lines are the same in this case as for the broken Life Line (sections 17 B 1, 2 and 3).

It is equally important not to confuse a *split* or branch in the Head Line with a broken Head Line. Splits are character markings discussed in Part Two.

25   *Abnormal Head Lines:* These are seen in the hands of congenital defectives. If the Head Line is absent in *both hands,* we are dealing with the so-called *Simian Line.*

25 A   *The Heart Line and Head Line are actually merged into one* and the infant is mentally doomed: This is one of the most easily confirmed aberrations.

25 B   *The Head Line is absent in one of the hands only:* This is not a common occurrence. The indication is that the marking is again a merged Heart and Head Line or a missing Heart Line, which is a character defect. I have not encountered any physical abnormalities in the few hands I have found so marked.

25 C   *The Head Line is made up of a chain, with many small islands, seemingly double and broad:* When seen in both hands, this is again the Head Line of the idiot, and is confirmed by the very small Thumb and usually the lack of a Heart Line (see Simian Line, section 25 A).

25 D   *The Head Line has many small hairlines crossing it:* This is usually found on the hand with many fine lines covering

[40]

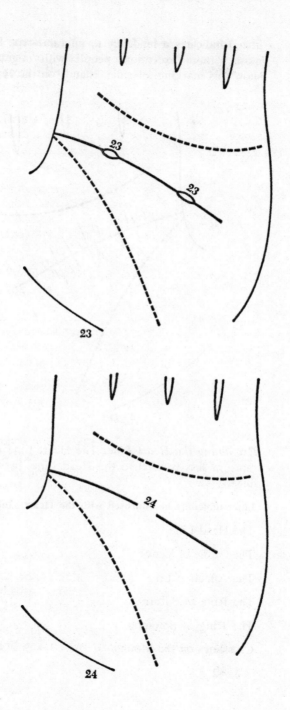

it and indicates a tendency to migraine-type headaches. Almost without exception, people with migraine headaches show this marking, or small islands on the Head Line.

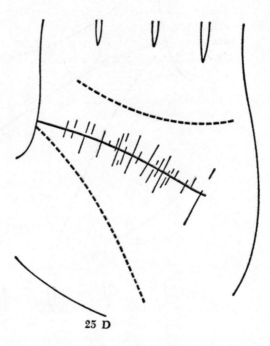

25 D

26 *Examining the Heart Line:* The Heart Line runs above and more or less parallel to the Head Line, between it and the fingers.

Lines that may be confused with the Heart Line

I personally do not use the Heart Line as an indication of events since these may be found more readily by examining the Affection Line, the Fate Line and the Life Line. It is worth examining the Heart Line as an indication of periods of affection, however, in much the same manner as we examine the Life Line for periods of physical strength and weakness. This requires a great deal of research, since the classical form of palmistry has not dealt with this aspect of the Heart Line to any extent.

I have sketched the various ages as marked on the Heart Line in the illustration to facilitate the examination. The Heart Line does not denote events, with three exceptions:

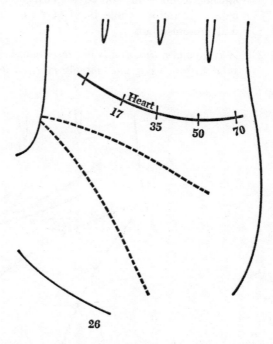

26

26 A   *The Heart Line with breaks:* Tells of a fatality causing the loss of a loved one.

26 B   *The Heart Line with islands:* This indicates heart disease *if* combined with an island on the Life Line.

26 B 1   According to one palmist who specializes in the interpretation of islands in the Heart Line, these islands indicate emotional attachments. The longer the island the more significant the attachment is in the life of the subject.

When the island is terminated by a line running into the Heart Line (from the percussion side of the island), it indicates that external conditions forced the termination of the relationship.

The location of the island under Apollo, blocking the Sun Line, means that the love partner made excessive demands, causing the subject great emotional and personal loss. According to this same source, the Affection Lines seem to indicate expectations while the Heart Line records actual past and present affairs.

26 B 2   *A companion line that is not terminated* indicates an ongoing relationship: Long and happily married individuals have this

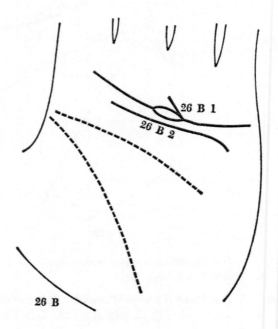

as a long parallel line running closely to the Heart Line for the duration of their life.

If the companion line veers out and away from the Heart Line, it indicates the "drifting apart" of the relationship.

26 B 3 *The companion line terminated by a line from or into the Heart Line:* Sudden termination of the relationship by external circumstances, causing great unhappiness. See also section 46 for confirming markings.

26 C *The Heart Line cuts through the Head Line:* This is a very bad sign when observed in the Major Hand. It indicates a very serious disease and usually death. See section 126, "Illness according to type," for particulars regarding the illness.

26 D *The Heart Line is missing in one or both hands:* This is considered a Simian Line (see section 25 A) or is covered in section 25 B, as in that case it cannot be verified which line is the remaining one.

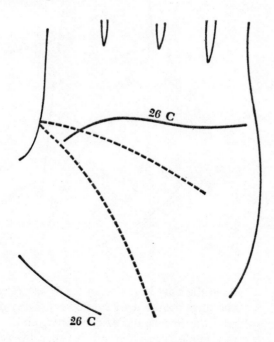

27   *Examining the Fate Line:* The Fate Line is the line that marks *all events pertaining to the worldly life* of the subject. It is a vertical line or series of lines running up the middle of the hand into the ring finger.

Lines that may be confused with the Fate Line

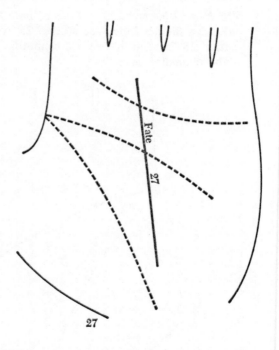

27

27 A   Read the Fate Line first in the *Minor Hand* (section 1): The markings denote the inherited capability of the subject. Then read the line in the *Major Hand,* and use the Major Hand as a guide. The difference between the two hands represents the qualitative change that the subject has made away from the inherited capability.

The Fate Line, as well as all lines from the wrist toward the fingers, is most prominent in certain types of hands: the long, narrow and pointed hand has many more marked upswept lines than the square hand. A well-marked Fate Line in the narrower, pointed hand is less effective than a thinly marked Fate Line in a square hand. When the amount of success is considered in this light, it will be seen that the square hand with the thin lines is equal to or more successful in achievement than the well-marked narrow hand. Also read section 49 for the Thumb, which influences worldly success. The quality of the Fate Line must be in proportion to the other lines to be a fair indicator of worldly success.

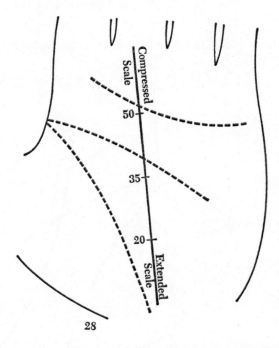

28

28   To read the *age* marked on the Fate Line, see illustration. It is easier to establish the age by asking the subject at what age a certain past event, which is shown on the line, occurred.

The other ages can immediately be derived from the given date by extrapolation.

29 *The origin of the Fate Line*

29 A *The Fate Line rises from the Thumb side of the Life Line:* This denotes a good early life, usually through the influence of the family.

29 B *The Fate Line rises from the Life Line itself:* When seen in both hands, this also denotes a good early life. If it continues as a strong line it marks success by personal achievement in all endeavors.

29 C *The Fate Line rises from the Mount of Luna:* When seen in both hands, it means that success is dependent upon other people. Many successful actors show the Fate Line to originate at this point.

29 D *The Fate Line rises from a point higher up in the palm:* This

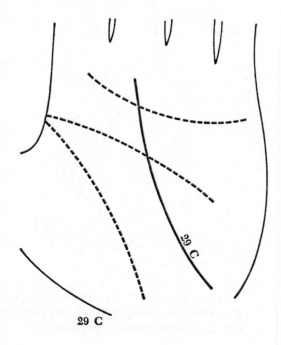

29 C

shows a later development of the capabilities, and success comes later in life.

The age is indicated by the starting point.

29 D 1 *Note:* When the Fate Line starts higher in the Major Hand than in the Minor Hand, the capabilities were not utilized at an early age.

29 E *Variations in the origin of the Fate Line*

29 E 1 The *Minor Fate Line* rises from Luna, the *Major Fate Line* rises from inside the Life Line: This combination is the sign of inherited capability based upon the influence of others, but the actual life was shielded by the family. This is seen in the hands of the subject whose parent is successful through the influence of others, accounting for the protection in childhood.

29 E 2 The *Minor Fate Line* rises from the center of the hand, the *Major Fate Line* rises from inside the Life Line: Again, early protection in childhood, but the parent is successful through own capabilities—as an inventor or a craftsman, for instance—in contrast to 29 E 1, where the parent was dependent on others for success.

29 E 3 The *Minor Fate Line* rises from inside the Life Line, the *Major Fate Line* from Luna: This is the reverse of 29 E 1. It denotes that the parents were shielded by the family and the subject is dependent on others for success. A typical example is a member of the foreign nobility who lost their wealth abroad.

29 E 4 The *Minor Fate Line* rises from inside the Life Line, the *Major Fate Line* rises from the center of the hand: This is the reverse of 29 E 2. It denotes that the parents were shielded by the family and the subject is self-made and successful. A typical example is the noble foreigner whose parents lost their wealth and who has made a success by his or her own inventiveness.

30 *The straight, unbroken Fate Line:* This is the best indication of worldly success. See the age markings for start and end of career life, and examine the origin of the Fate Line (section 29) for the source of success.

31   *The Fate Line with breaks:* This indicates a loss or misfortune in worldly endeavors paired with a great change. Repair signs are the same as for the Life Line (sections 17 B 1, 2, 3). The continuation of the line, if any, indicates the nature and direction of change.

The distance between the broken portions of the Fate Line indicates the amount of change that takes place. The wider the break, the greater the change.

The Minor and Major Fate Lines will often be markedly different. The *Major Fate Line* represents the life of the *subject;* the Minor Fate Line indicates what the potential of the subject is at the various ages.

This is a very important point, because the subject can at choice follow the inherited trait, provided the willpower as indicated by the first phalanx of the Thumb is sufficiently strong (see section 49).

31 A   *Direction of change* of the broken Fate Line is indicated by the course of the continuation:

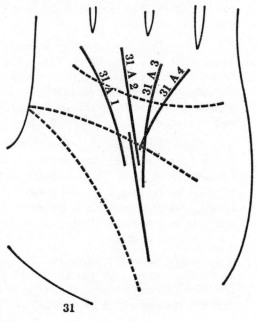

31

31 A 1   *The broken Fate Line continues to the Index Finger (Jupiter):* If the broken line continues before the previous portion of the Fate Line terminates, a matter of being personally honored is indicated.

31 A 2   *The broken Fate Line continues to the Middle Finger (Saturn):* This indicates a change of position, with attendant success. If the broken line continues before the previous portion of the Fate Line terminates, the change is by choice of the subject and will be successful.

31 A 3   *The broken Fate Line continues to the Ring Finger (Apollo):* This indicates that the change is into the arts. If the broken line continues before the previous portion of the Fate Line terminates, the change comes by personal choice with attendant success.

31 A 4   *The broken Fate Line continues to the Little Finger (Mercury):* This indicates that the subject will follow a career in science from the age indicated at the start of the break. If the broken line continues before the previous portion of the Fate Line has terminated, the change comes by personal choice with attendant success.

32   *Doubling of the Fate Line:* This indicates more than one career and is an excellent sign. Do not confuse the Sun Line (section 38) with a sister line to the Fate Line.

32 A   *Companion lines to the Fate Line:* This is not to be confused with the double Fate Line. A companion line is a very fine line, like a hairline, very closely following a portion or all of the Fate Line. This indicates a close personal relationship or affection for someone.

33   *Branches from the Fate Line*

33 A   *A branch from the Fate Line to the Index Finger* (Jupiter): At the age indicated on the Fate Line, this means unusual success in personal achievement.

33 B   *A branch from the Fate Line to the Ring Finger* (Apollo): Unusual success in the arts at the age indicated.

33 C   *A branch from the Fate Line to the Little Finger* (Mercury): Unusual success in business and science at the age indicated.

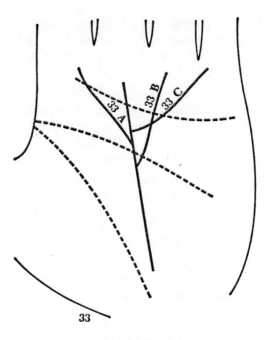

33

34 *Branches to the Fate Line:* These are lines rising from the wrist to the fingers, joining the Fate Line. In dealing with branches to the Fate Line, we must consider the starting point of the branch.

All branches to the Fate Line help the worldly success at the age as read on the Fate Line.

Do not confuse a joining branch with a crossing line, which is a negative mark. Note that all branches must *join* the Fate Line, not cross or break it.

34 A *The branch originates on the Thumb side of the Life Line,* smoothly crossing the Life Line and joining the Fate Line: As with the Fate Line originating on Venus (see section 29 A), this indicates help from the subject's family, but the hand denotes great promise, even without such help, since the success marking is there as a personal characteristic.

34 B *The branch joining the Fate Line originates between the Life Line and the Fate Line:* This area of origin is called middle

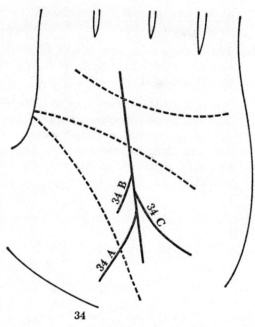

34

Mars. This means that the success is not caused by other people but by a mechanical device.

It does not originate in the mind of the person, but is arrived at by chance. If this means an invention, it was not the item that the inventor was looking for; it was come upon serendipitously.

34 C *The branch joining the Fate Line originates on the Mount of Luna:* This indicates success, but with the help of other people not in the family. It is a stronger marking than the Fate Line ascending from the area of Luna, since it does not make the success wholly dependent on others.

35 *Markings on the Fate Line:* Misfortunes are also marked on the Fate Line, meaning financial and business losses.

35 A *The chained Fate Line* in the Major Hand: This indicates a time of hardship in worldly affairs. It is better than a total absence of Fate Line during the period.

35 A 1 *The chained Major Fate Line with a solid Minor Fate Line* at the same period: The potential is there, but external conditions make it impossible for the subject to achieve success.

35 A 2 *The chained Fate Line* in the Minor Hand: This indicates that the inherited capability is lacking at the particular age period indicated.

35 A 3 *The chained Minor Fate Line* with the *solid Major Fate Line:* The enormous willpower of the subject is obvious, as evidenced by the strong Thumb (section 49) or an Influence Line branching into the Fate Line (section 34) showing outside help at that point. Success would not normally be expected.

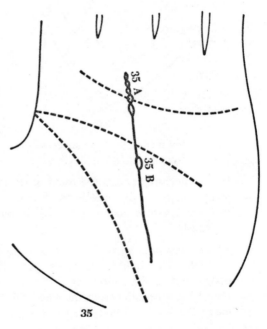

35

35 B *The Fate Line with islands:* Islands in the Fate Line indicate a loss. If the island is connected with a fork in the Fate Line or with a line that sweeps up to the Fate Line and touches it, this indicates a loss through a lawsuit or family problem.

35 C *Lines smoothly crossing the Fate Line* are indications of problems encountered in the career of the person.

Note: These lines must cross smoothly, and must not be composed of one line joining and another line leaving the Fate Line. *If a great number of fine hairlines* are seen crossing the Fate Line, disregard them as event markings. These are discussed in section 12.

35 C 1 *The origin* of the line smoothly crossing the Fate Line is *on the Thumb side of the Life Line:* This line is read on the Life Line, not on the Fate Line, and it affects life, not the career (see section 12).

35 C 2 *The origin* of the line smoothly crossing the Fate Line is *from the Life Line:* This line is read as above, affecting life, not the career.

35 C 3 *The origin* of the line smoothly crossing the Fate Line is from the palm, *thumbside of the Fate Line,* between the Life and Fate Lines: This indicates a problem encountered in the career.

If the Fate Line continues normally, the problem is of limited duration.

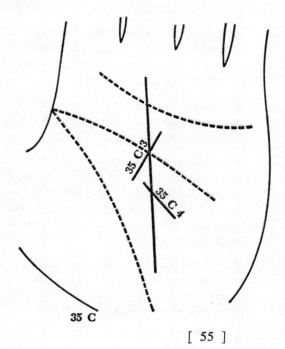

35 C

If the Fate Line at this point *breaks and changes,* the problem forces the subject into another career. The new career is determined by the direction of change of the Fate Line (see section 31 A).

35 C 4 *The origin* of the line smoothly crossing the Fate Line is from the *percussion side of the Fate Line* and is not a branch to the Fate Line (section 34): In looking for such crossing lines, read only very short lines starting at the percussion side and ending very close to the Fate Line:

This indicates that the imagination—overestimating oneself—has created the career problem. Not serious if the Fate Line continues normally.

35 D *Repair lines in the Fate Line:* The misfortunes marked in the Fate Line are financial and career problems. The repair mark preserves the subject from the consequences of the misfortune.

35 D 1 *A square* on the Fate Line preserves the subject at the point where a discontinuation of the Fate Line occurs.

36 *Absence of the Fate Line:* The hand without a Fate Line denotes a character failing and is discussed in Part Two, section 116 B. It does not denote so much a lack of success as a lack of inherited good fortune.

37 *Termination of the Fate Line* by the *Head Line:* This indicates that success is ruined by a mental miscalculation, if the line does not continue elsewhere.

37 A *Termination of the Fate Line* by the *Heart Line:* This indicates that the successful career is ruined by an emotional upheaval. Note, however, that when the Fate Line runs into the Heart Line, joins it and continues toward the Index Finger (Jupiter), this means very great success in the most ambitious undertakings.

38 *Examining the Sun Line:* The Sun Line is the indicator of creative success of the individual and is of importance to all aspiring artists. It is another vertical line, found under the Ring Finger (Apollo).

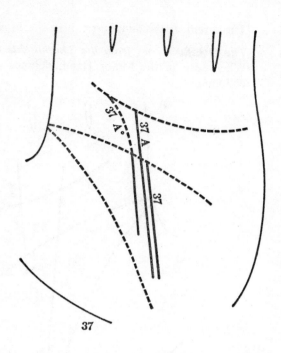

37

Lines that may be confused with the Sun Line

Event markings on the Sun Line are identical to those on the Fate Line (sections 35 and 35 A) but refer to the creative rather than the business aspect of events.

When the required success is wholly in the arts, the Sun Line substitutes for the Fate Line.

See section 27 A to read the Sun Line in the Minor and Major Hands, which follows the consideration for the Fate Line.

38 A   *The Sun Line rises from the Thumb side of the Life Line:* When seen in the Major Hand, denotes a protected early childhood.

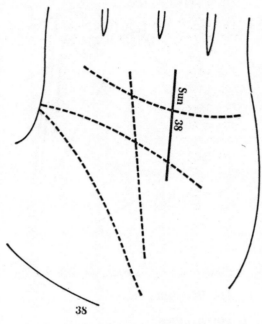

38

38 B   *The Sun Line rises from the Life Line itself* in the Major Hand: This marks the best possible start for the artist. It denotes personal capabilities beyond inherited talent.

38 C   *The Sun Line rises from the center of the hand:* This is the normal start mark for the Sun Line. It lends the creative talent required by the artist. See the Thumb for supporting willpower (section 49).

38 D   *The Sun Line rises from a point higher up in the palm:* Indicates a later development of the creative capabilities. Success comes later in life.

38 E   *The Sun Line rises from the Fate Line:* This is considered a branch from the Fate Line to the Ring Finger, and denotes success in the arts. The age is read on the Fate Line.

38 F   *Variations in the origin* of the Sun Line

38 F 1   *The Major Sun Line rises from the Mount of Luna:* Indicates that success in the arts depends on the help of others (see also 29 E 3). The artist is pushed to success without much personal effort.

38 F 2   *The Major Sun Line rises from the Head Line:* Indicates that the success is wholly self-made through no outside help, but the success is achieved later in life.

38 F 3   *The Major Sun Line rises from the Heart Line:* Indicates an appreciation for the arts, developing at a later part of life.

38 F 4   *The Major Sun Line rises very low in the hand,* with Ring Finger and Middle Finger equally long: With a weak thumb (section 49), this makes a gambler; with a strong thumb, a patron of the arts.

38 G   *The straight, unbroken Sun Line:* The best indication of creative success. The position of the origin must be carefully noted for the start of the career (section 38 A through F).

38 H   *The Sun Line with breaks:* Indicates a stop-and-go type of

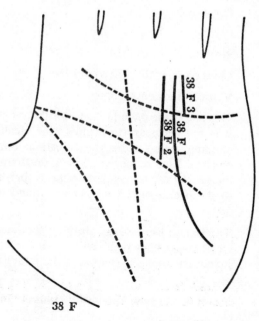

38 F

artistic career. Compare this with section 31 to determine the variations in the artistic career. Age is determined as on the Fate Line.

38 I   *Doubling of the Sun Line:* Indicates a multiple arts career and is usually encountered in a hand filled with many vertical lines, as explained in section 27 A. Do not confuse the double line with the Fate Line.

38 J   *Branches from and to the Sun Line:* These are treated like those on the Fate Line, but affecting the creative career. See sections 33 and 34.

38 K   *The Sun Line with islands:* Indicates a loss of position or a loss of name, for an artist. The age at which the loss occurs is read as on the Fate Line.

38 L   *Absence of the Sun Line:* Indicates a total lack of recognition for the artist. The talent may be there, but no success will follow.

39   *Examining the Health Line* or Hepatica

Lines that may be confused with the Health Line

Portions of the Life Line . . . . section 3

Portions of the Fate Line . . . . section 27, 29

Portions of the Sun Line . . . . section 38

Lines crossing the Affection Line . . . . section 46 B

Vertical lines on Mercury . . . . section 119 C 4

This line is the main indicator of the subject's physical health. It is not necessary to evaluate the Health Line as an event marking, unless there are indications on the Life Line and/ or Head Line requiring a check on the physical condition of the subject at various parts of his or her life. Additional clues to the health of the subject are found in the nails (section 50).

The Health Line is read starting from the Little Finger (Mercury) down toward the wrist. It is one of the most important influences upon the success of the total hand since it indicates any physical weakness that will handicap life.

We also can read the Health Line as the so-called *Mercury*

[60]

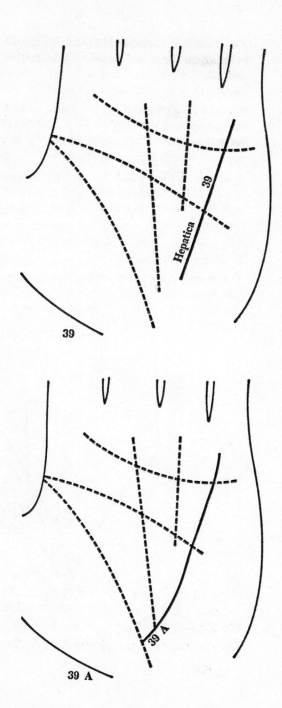

Hepatica

39

39 A

Line, which is found in the hands of those who are successful in sales, business and science but who have a weak digestion and are subject to ulcers and gall and kidney stones. See Mount of Mercury (section 110 D).

39 A   *The juncture of the Hepatica and Life Line* usually indicates the life-span of the subject: This indicates the age of the natural termination of life, as read on the Life Line. This must appear in both hands, however, to serve as an indicator.

40   *Absence of the Health Line:* This is an indication of *good health.* If the Life Line and Head and Heart Lines are equally well formed, this is a sure indication of a life without major illnesses.

41   *The starting position of the Health Line* indicates the type of illness encountered.

41 A   *The Health Line starts at the Little Finger:* Starting at a point just under the Little Finger (Mercury) and going into or through the Life Line, it foretells heart disease or circulatory weakness.

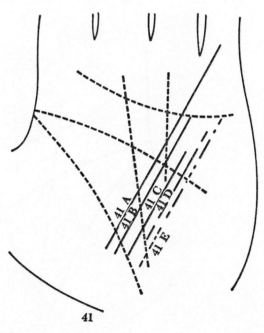

41

41 B   *The Health Line starts from the Heart Line:* This is also an indicator of heart disease and can be counterchecked with the nails (section 50).

41 C   *The Health Line starts in the middle of the hand* and goes to or through the Life Line: Indicates worsening health at a later age.

41 D   *The Health Line starts and stops intermittently:* Generally indicates a form of physical weakness at the age shown on the Life Line.

41 E   *The Health Line consists of small interrupted sections:* Indicates a problem in the digestive system.

42   *Deformations of the Health Line:* The deformation of this line is a reliable clue to the type of physical weakness. Take the information in both hands, using the Major Hand as guide to the subject. As is the case with the other lines, the Minor Hand indicates the inherited trend.

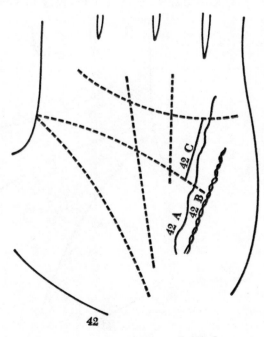

42 A *A twisting Health Line:* Indicates a tendency to liver or gall-bladder troubles. In this case, the line must also be made up of little pieces and poorly marked.

42 B *The Health Line made up of little islands* is a clue to lung disease.

42 C *If the Health Line is deeply marked* only between the Head and Heart Lines, it indicates mental disturbance. (This will be also shown as an island on the Head Line.)

43 *The Affection or Marriage Line:* The Marriage Line has its own *age indication* by reading from the Heart Line to the Little Finger. The closer it is found to the Heart Line, the younger the affection occurs. The important factor is that we can read the number of major affections and the age at which they occur by considering the center to be at 24 or 25 years of age.

This line is one of the least understood lines in the hand since so many palmists found it hard to interpret the meanings. Cheiro considers these lines only in connection with many

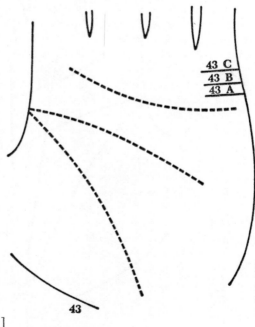

other markings in the hand to come to a final conclusion; Psychos takes a similar view and accepts even close ties between family members as reason for these markings. Desbarolles was more positive in his views as to it meaning marriage, but he lived under quite different circumstances in a deeply religious society. I examine the line as a matter of routine since my main interest is of course in the event lines of the past and their constancy of meaning. My interpretation is usually of a general nature, and I will tell the subject that the selection of a life or love partner occurs at about such and such an age.

43 A   When the Affection Line is located close to the Heart Line it indicates age 14 up to 17.

43 B   When the line is *centered between the Heart Line and Little Finger,* the age indicated is about 24 years.

43 C   Three quarters up is about 30 years of age.

44   Since the Affection Line indicates a major relationship only, other lines will be equally strong as indications of the period at which the influence over the person is exerted. See the Life Line and Fate Line for Companion Lines. See also section 18 B.

45   *Divorce* is indicated by a break in the *Marriage Line,*

45 A   by the *disappearance of a Companion Line to the Life Line,*

45 B   or by its *merging with the Life Line after running alongside it.* If a more complete change of life is connected with the divorce, a repaired break in the Life Line may be seen in the Major Hand.

46   *Markings on the Affection Line:* The best form of Affection Line is a straight, unbroken line, indicating an even, happy relationship.

46 A   *The end of the Affection Line* (away from the edge of the hand) *curves upward:* This makes it improbable that the person will make a permanent alliance.

46 A 1   *The end of the Affection Line curves downward:* This means that the partner will die first.

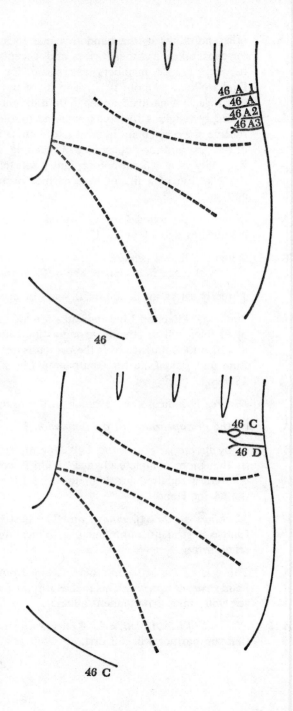

46

46 A 1
46 A
46 A 2
46 A 3

46 C
46 D

46 C

46 A 2 *The end of the Affection Line is broken:* The sign of divorce or separation.

46 A 3 *The end of the Affection Line has a cross marked on it:* The partner will die in an accident.

46 B *Hairlines drop through the Affection Line:* This indicates poor health in the partner.

46 C The Affection Line with *islands:* This indicates great trouble in the relationship, also easily verified in the Life and Fate Lines where it is shown as a crossing Line (see sections 12 A, 12 C).

46 D *A forked ending of the Affection Line:* This is a negative marking in the relationship.

47 *Multiplicity of Affection Lines:* Many hands carry more than one Affection Line. In this case it is important to check the Life Line and Fate Line for Companion Lines, at the approximate age. The exact period of the affection is given on the Life or Fate lines (section 18 B and 32 A).

48 *Companion markings to events:* The event marks found in the hand, on the Life Line, the Fate Line, the Sun Line and the Health and Affection Lines, as determined in sections 1 to 48 are modified in a number of ways.

49 *The Thumb as it modifies event markings:* When worldly success is noted in the Fate Line, the amount of success is largely dependent on the *willpower and logic* of the subject.

49 A *Willpower* is determined by the first phalanx (nail phalanx) of the Thumb: If the first phalanx is long, it indicates strong willpower.

49 B *Logic* is indicated by the second phalanx of the Thumb: A long second phalanx indicates logic; a short one, a lack of logical thinking.

49 C *Determining the amount of worldly success:* A strong first phalanx reaches success through willpower; a strong second phalanx, through logic.

49 D *The type of success* is determined by the direction of the Success Lines (section 33) and the direction of the Fate Line itself (section 27 and 31 A).

50   *Determination of illnesses and disorders:* Read the *Health Line* as explained in sections 39 through 42. If the Life Line is deformed (*chained* or *tasseled*) along part or most of its way, use the Health Line and nails to determine the illness and physical weakness of the subject. Also see Part Two, section 126, "Illnesses according to type."

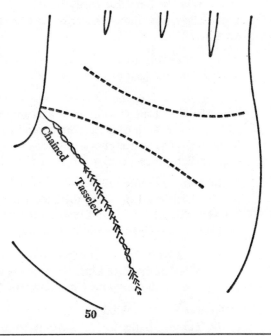

50

Nail markings confirm the findings on the Health Line.

We can obtain very precise information about the health of the subject even without consulting the Health Line. For this reason it is important to note or sketch the shape of the nails in the palm print. The variations in nail form occur in the following areas:

50 A   *The long nail* is an indication of chest and lung trouble: Generally speaking, the long nail denotes a person who physically is not quite as strong as the person with short nails.

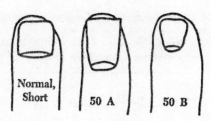

Normal, Short | 50 A | 50 B

50 B   *The short, small nail* indicates a tendency to heart disease in later age: Generally speaking, the *short nail* belongs to a group of people who suffer from intestinal, circulatory and lower back and leg problems; the *long-nail* group suffers in the upper part of the body, lungs and head.

50 C   When an abnormal *color or shape* is observed in the nails, we can expect a hereditary health defect:

The *lack of moons* at the base of the nail is a sign of poor blood circulation; the same defect is shown by the extremely bluish appearance of the entire nail.

50 D   The *surface* of the nails should be smooth and even: When fluting is encountered, with ridges running the length of the nail, we are dealing with a nervous respiratory disorder. This is commonly encountered in people who are sensitive to polluted air or allergic in general.

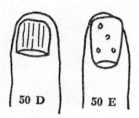

50 D | 50 E

50 E   *White spots on the nails* are seen in the highly nervous personality and usually correspond with a very large number of fine lines crossing the entire palm.

50 F   If the Health Line and nails indicate physical weakness, and if the Life Line carries an illness mark in the form of an island, dot or spot, it denotes a more acute form of illness than the Health Line and nails alone will indicate.

[69]

50 G   *The island in the Life Line* indicates a prolonged illness.

50 H   *The spot in the Life Line* indicates an acute attack on the nervous system, caused by surgery or strong medication.

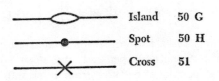

Island	50 G
Spot	50 H
Cross	51

51   *A cross modifying an event mark:* The cross is a negative marking. It consists of two lines crossing separately, not formed by other lines crossing by chance due to their nature. The point where the major lines cross each other is not considered a cross.

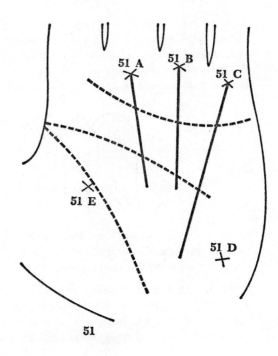

Note: There are no meanings to *fine chance lines* crossing each other. *The nervous hand has many of these hairlines.*

The cross is a warning sign to be read as follows:

51 A   *The cross touches the Fate Line* under the Middle Finger: This indicates danger of death by accident.

51 B   *The cross touches the Sun Line* under the Ring Finger: This indicates bad ending of an artistic career.

51 C   *The cross touches the Health Line* under the Little Finger: This indicates bankruptcy and failure of business and scientific endeavor.

51 D   *The cross on the Mount of Luna:* A complete mental breakdown is shown in this mark, especially when touching the Head Line.

51 E   *The cross on the area thumbside from the Life Line* (Venus): When distinctly marked, the cross touching the Life Line means trouble in the family life.

52   *A grille modifying an event mark:* The grille is a character modification unless the Fate or Sun Line terminates in a grille. This negates the power of the line and is a bad sign for the eventual success of the individual.

53   *A triangle modifying an event mark:* The triangle is a *positive* marking. It reinforces the qualities of the person. It is not made by the chance crossing of lines, and stands out clearly by itself.

It is a character marking unless the Fate, Head or Sun Lines terminate in or very near the clearly marked triangle.

Grille 52

Triangle 53

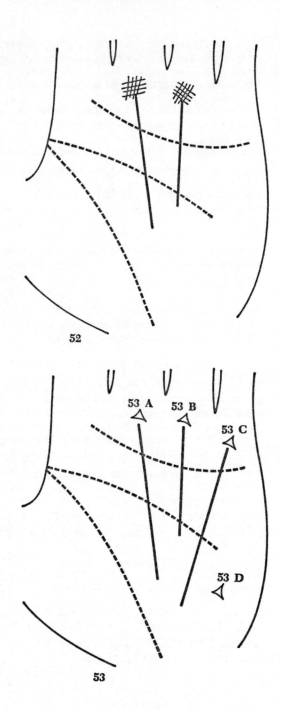

52

53

53 A *The Fate Line terminates at or near a clearly marked triangle:* The individual will excel at management of people and organization. This mark must be accompanied by a strong Thumb (section 49) for fullest effect.

53 B *The Sun Line terminates at or near a clearly marked triangle:* The individual is an accomplished practical artist. See also Thumb marking above.

53 C *The Health Line starts at or near a clearly marked triangle* under the Little Finger: This indicates that the person will be highly successful in business or the sciences.

53 D *The triangle clearly marked on Luna:* This sign, found in the hand of inventors and acknowledged authors, denotes great success in the use of the imagination. The Head Line should come close to the triangle for maximum effect.

54 *A square modifying an event mark:* A clearly marked square not formed by chance crossing of lines is a *preservation mark* except as in 54 B.

Square   54

54 A *Any line running through a square* is preserved from a negative event mark shown within the square.

54 B *The square touches or is very close* to the Life Line on the thumbside of the Life Line, not over the Life Line: This indicates isolation from society. This sign is seen in prisoners and those who were isolated for health reasons.

SECONDARY LINES AND MARKINGS

These are the event lines and character-modifying lines. To help recognize them, I have prepared nine maps showing the event lines discussed in Part One, sections 1 through 61.

In comparing the actual hand or hand print with the chart area, eliminate from the area the primary lines already discussed. This will leave only the secondary markings, which are event and character marks.

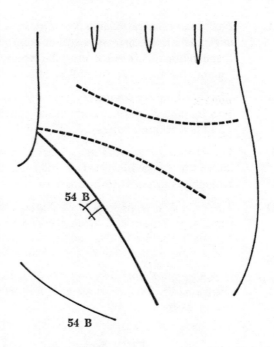

54 B

It is of the utmost importance in the evaluation of event marks and event lines to know the meaning of the areas where these lines start and stop.

By dividing the hand under each finger into three equal sections from finger to wrist, we get 12 areas where event lines can originate or terminate:

* *First Tier*
  The areas of Jupiter, Saturn, Apollo and Mercury

* *Second Tier*
  The four areas of Mars

* *Third Tier*
  The four areas of Venus and Luna

Some markings sometimes have been omitted from the charts for reasons of clarity: the *grille* and the *event line with islands* are examples, but these will be discussed under the event line or character mark in question. There are also *hands covered with fine lines,* these again are not shown on the charts. For that explanation, see section 12.

The lines with numbers up to and including 61 are *event markings.* Numbers 101 and up are character markings. Write down the numbers found alongside each line that has been properly identified. If the number is between 1 and 61 inclusive, find out where the line crosses the Life Line, the Fate Line or the Sun Line. This crossing point gives the age indication. In some cases, the low number line does not cross a major line, but then the *age* will be implied by the position of the line, as explained in the section covering that line. (See section 43, Affection Line, as an example.) If the low number is connected with a *mark* rather than a line, the explanation will be given in the section itself.

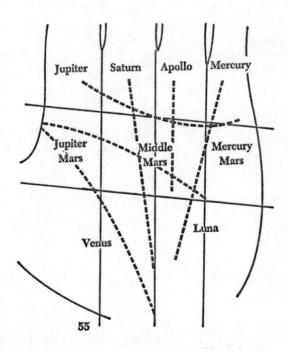

Area A 1, Jupiter, located directly under the Index Finger.

If a secondary line is found in Area A 1: See sections 10 A 2, 12, 31 A 1, 33 A, 55, 114 A, 114 A 3, 115 A, 115 A 1, 115 A 2, 115 A 3, 115 B 3, 115 D 1, 115 H, 118 B, 118 C, 118 D, 119 A 1, 119 B 1, 119 C 1, 120 A 1, 123 A

Some of these secondary lines are:

* *vertical lines* (119 C 1)

* *horizontal lines* (120 A 1)

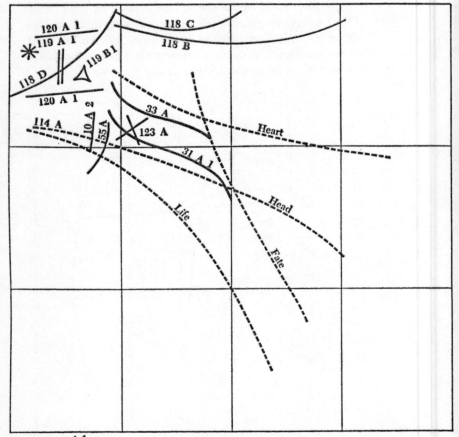

A 1

*   *Terminating and originating* lines that connect with other areas (10 A 2, 55 A, etc.) or

*   *Special Jupiter markings* (118 D, 119 A 1, etc.)

Note: Only one of the possible positions is given. Each of the lines that is shown may be located anywhere in the Jupiter area, but must bear the same character. For instance, a horizontal line anywhere in the Jupiter area, which does not *leave* this area, is read as *120 A 1*. Similarly, any vertical line that does not leave the Jupiter Area A 1 is read as *119 C 1*.

Line marking 116 A from the Fate Line to the Jupiter area may terminate anywhere in that area. Normally there are far fewer lines in the Jupiter area, since most possible lines have been drawn in on the chart.

The general rule is that all *negative* lines ending on Jupiter are *restrictive* in matters of religion, ambition and honor.

All positive lines ending on Jupiter augur well in matters of religion, ambition and honor.

55 A   *An event line ends in the area of Jupiter after crossing the area of Mars and the Life Line and having originated on the area of Venus:* This is in the group of negative lines described in section 12. The ending of the line in Jupiter denotes that the person has been forced by close relatives into a restrictive position involving religion or the army at the age indicated.

55 B   *An event line ends in the area of Jupiter, after having crossed the area of Mars and originating from the Life Life:* This is in the group of positive lines described in section 10 A.

The result is typical of the area of Jupiter: ambitions that are realized. The *religions* are strong on Jupiter, and in a practical hand it can be assumed that the leadership is in the church.

Love of nature is a Jupiterian character trait, and with this hand an ecologist can be recognized.

If the entire hand is very dominating with a very strong Thumb, the choice is *church;* in a philosophic hand, the choice is *nature.*

55 C   *An event line ends in the area of Jupiter originating in the*

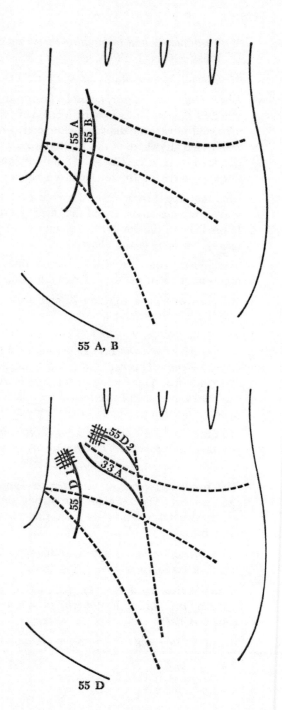

55 A, B

55 D

Fate Line: A branch from the Fate Line to the area of Jupiter, section 33 A, means that a personal ambition is achieved.

55 D   *An event line ends in the area of Jupiter with a grille formation.*

55 D 1   *Originating on Venus:* Restrictions for faith reasons: the convent, the close family thwarts the ambition. Age is indicated on the Life Line.

55 D 2   *Originating from the Fate Line:* The dethroned leader, blocked success, dishonor. Age is indicated on the Fate Line.

56   *Area A 2, Saturn, is located under the Middle Finger.*

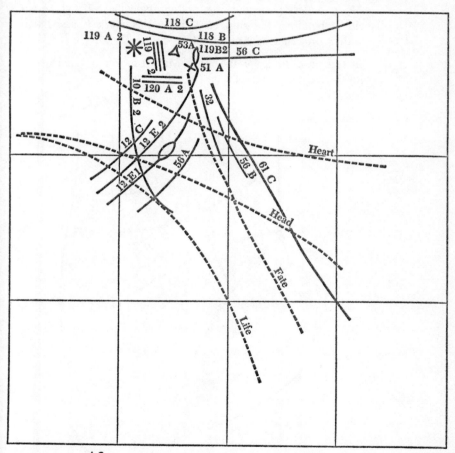

A 2

If a secondary line is found in Area A 2: See sections 10 B 2, 12, 12 B, 12 C, 12 D, 12 E, 12 E 1, 12 E 2, 32, 32 A, 51 A, 53 A, 56 A, 56 B, 56 C, 114 D 2, 115 F 4, 118 B, 118 C, 119 A 2, 119 B 2, 119 C 2, 119 D 3, 120 A 2

The general rule is that all *negative* lines ending on Saturn are misfortunes, *very severe accidents* or incidents. The positive lines ending on Saturn are successful markings, as is the termination of the Fate Line, in that area.

56 A *An event line ends in the area of Saturn originating in the area of Venus, and smoothly crossing the Life and Head Lines:* A very poor marking, noting a specific, very grave accident befalling the subject. Usually this mark is associated with a broken Life Line or Head Line.

In this case, look for the inner Mars Line or a square over the break, as repair marks.

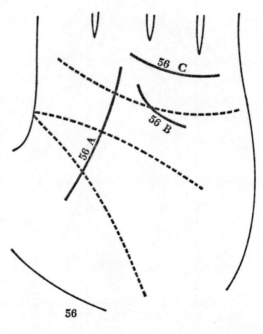

56

56 B *An event line ends in the area of Saturn and originates in the area of Mars:* Do not confuse with the Fate Line or with sister lines to the Fate Line.

This marks an accident caused by a mechanical device. If the Life Line and Head Line show no definite unrepaired breaks, the marking is not fatal.

56 C *An event line ends in the area of Saturn originating in the area of Mercury:* If the Line of Affection is the source, a fatality involving the marriage is indicated.

If the area of origin is the inner area of Mercury, a fatality in an athletic event is indicated.

Note Life and Head Lines for additional information.

---

57 *Area A 3, Apollo, is located directly under the Ring Finger.*

If a secondary line is found in Area A 3: See sections 10 C 2, 12 D, 33 B, 38 I, 51 B, 53 B, 57 A, 57 B, 114 D 3, 115 D 3, 115 F 4, 118 A, 118 B, 119 A 3, 119 B 3, 119 C 3, 120 A 3

The general rule is that all *positive* event lines on Apollo indicate personal achievements in the creative arts; all *negative* event lines involve failures in achievement.

The area of Apollo has a second indication, namely the *physical eye.* Eye injury is seen in a deformation in the Sun Line or on the area of Apollo.

57 A *Event lines end in the area of Apollo originating from the area of Venus:* With a break in the Head Line, it indicates an eye injury. Without a break on the Head Line, it denotes a great loss in personal effort through a close relative. Age is indicated on the Life Line. This is a typical example of the variation in an event line caused by the addition of one single factor. Whenever I encounter an event line starting on Venus (thumbside from the Life Line), then cutting the Life Line, the Fate Line, the Head Line and the Heart Line, and finally ending on Apollo or Mercury, there is cause for carefully checking the Head Line. The fact that the event line

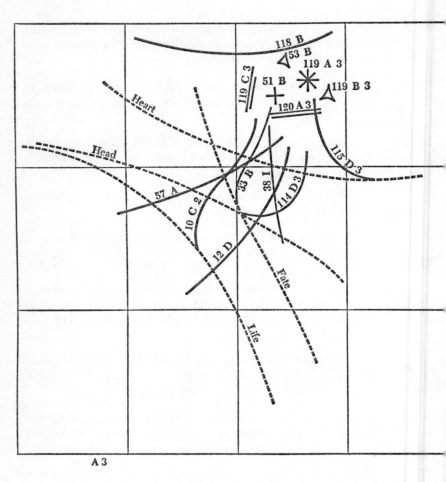

A 3

cuts through all the major lines in itself is questionable. In the case of the Apollo termination, I immediately check the Head Line again for a break, which would indicate that the eye is involved.

On the first examination of the major lines (the primary step in all analysis), the minor break in the Head Line might have escaped attention. A careful scrutiny with a magnifier must be made after such an event line is found.

When I can find no sign of break on the Head Line, I tell

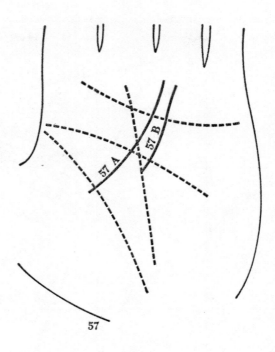

57

the subject that at the given age, great opposition was encountered from the family in an art or business venture.

57 B   *Event lines end in the area of Apollo, originating in the Fate Line:* These are success markings. See section 33 B.

Also see branches from the Life Line, section 10 C.

---

58   *Area A 4, Mercury, is located directly under the Small Finger.*

If a secondary line is found in Area A 4: See sections 10 D 2, 33 C, 43, 45, 46, 46 A, 46 B, 46 C, 46 D, 47, 51 C, 53 C, 56 C, 58 A, 58 B, 114 D 4, 115 D 4, 115 F 4, 118 A, 118 B, 119 A 4, 119 B 4, 119 C 4, 120 A 4

The two types of events noted on Mercury are those relating to business and athletic achievements and those with reference to the affections.

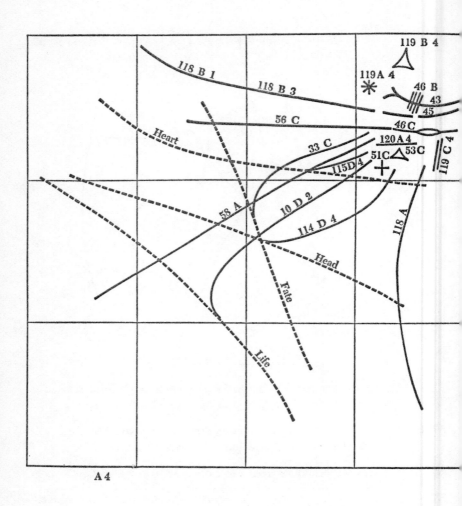

A 4

The notations regarding Affection Lines are contained in section 43.

58 A   *Event lines end in the area of Mercury originating in the area of Venus:* A big disillusionment, thwarted effort in business, by a close relation, at age indicated on the Life Line.

58 B   *Event lines end in the area of Mercury originating in the Life or Fate Lines:* For Success Lines, see sections 10 D 2 and

33 C. Do not confuse the Health Line with one of these event lines. Success at that late age marking is seen only on the Fate Line.

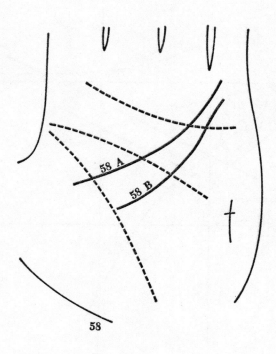

59

Areas B 1–4, Mars—event notations on Major Hand only:

If a secondary line is found in Area B 1: See sections 10 A 1, 11 A, 18 B, 51 E, 55 A, 55 D 1, 58 A, 59 A, 115 F 4, 119 A 5, 119 A 7, 119 B 6, 119 E, 119 F, 122, 123 A

If a secondary line is found in Area B 2: See sections 10 A 1, 10 B 1, 10 C 1, 10 D 1, 11 A, 11 C, 12, 12 A, 12 B, 12 C, 18 B 1, 25 D, 33 A, 33 B, 34 A, 34 B, 35 C 3, 35 C 4, 35 D 1, 54 B, 56 B, 59 A, 59 A 1, 114 D, 114 D 2, 114 D 3, 114 D 4, 114 D 7, 114 E, 119 A 5, 119 E, 119 F 1, 123 A, 123 B, 123 C

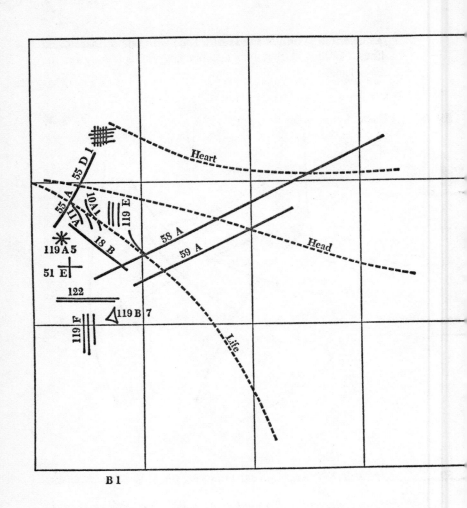

B 1

If a secondary line is found in Area B 3: See sections 10 C, 10 C 2, 10 D 1, 10 D 2, 12 A, 12 B, 12 C, 12 D, 12 E, 12 E 1, 25 D, 31, 31 A 1, 31 A 2, 31 A 3, 31 A 4, 32, 32 A, 33 B, 33 C, 34, 35 C 1, 35 C 2, 35 C 3, 35 C 4, 38 J, 51 B, 59 A, 59 A 1, 114 D 2, 114 D 3, 114 D 4, 114 D 5, 114 D 6, 114 E, 115 D 4, 118 A, 119 A 5, 119 B 5, 119 D 3, 119 D 4, 119 E, 123 B

If a secondary line is found in Area B 4: See sections 42 B, 42 C, 114 D 5, 118 A, 119 A 5, 119 B 5, 119 D

The area of Mars denotes mechanical products and warlike events.

59 A   *Event lines end in the area of Mars originating in the area of Venus:* A close relation destroys an effort through an act of aggression.

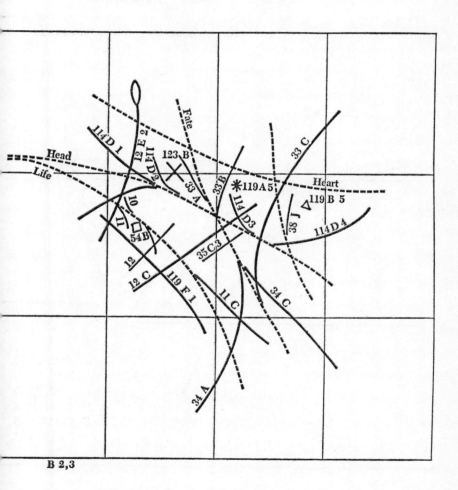

B 2,3

Note: This sign appears also in the case of a close relation suffering from an act of aggression. The difference is seen in the Fate Line notation, same age, which will be unbroken in the latter case.

59 A 1 *An event line ends in the area of Mars originating in the area of Venus, with a break in the Life Line:* A fatal act of war committed against the person. Merely an accident if the broken Life Line is in the Minor Hand only.

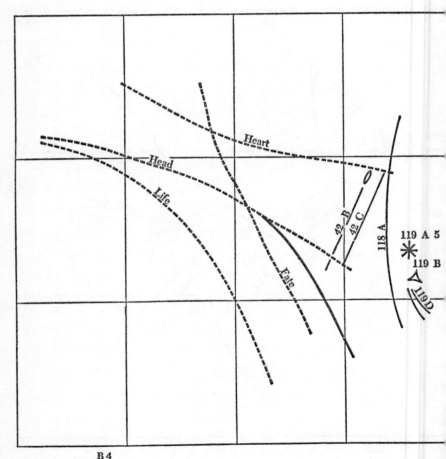

B 4

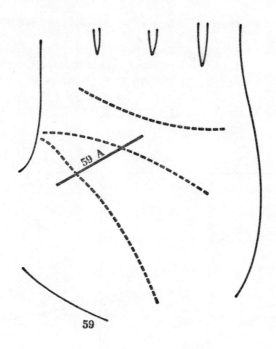

59 A

59

60   *Area C 1 and C 2, Venus—event notations in the Major Hand:*

If a secondary line is found in Area C 1: See sections 10, 11, 12, 17 B 1, 34 A, 34 B, 35 C 1, 51 E, 57 A, 58 A, 59 A, 59 A 1, 119 A 7, 119 B 7, 119 F, 122 A, 122 B, 122 C

If a secondary line is found in Area C 2: See sections 10, 11, 12, 18 B 1, 32 A, 34 A, 34 B, 35 C 3, 38 J, 51 E, 54 B, 57 A, 58 A, 58 B, 59 A, 59 A 1, 119 A 7, 119 B 7, 119 F, 122, 122 A, 122 B, 122 C

This part of the hand is the later life indication. Lines that originate in this area are read as in section 12.

In general, any lines originating in this area are the Fate and Sun Lines; it is the ending area for the Life Line.

61   *Areas C 3 and C 4, Luna—event notations in the Major Hand:*

If a secondary line is found in Area C 3: See sections 10 A, 10 B 1, 10 C 1, 10 D 1, 11 A, 11 B, 11 C, 18 B 1, 32 A, 34 A, 34 B, 34 C, 35 C 4, 38 I, 38 J, 41 D, 42 B, 51 D, 53 D, 114 D 5, 114 D 6, 118 A, 119 A 6, 119 B 5, 119 D, 121

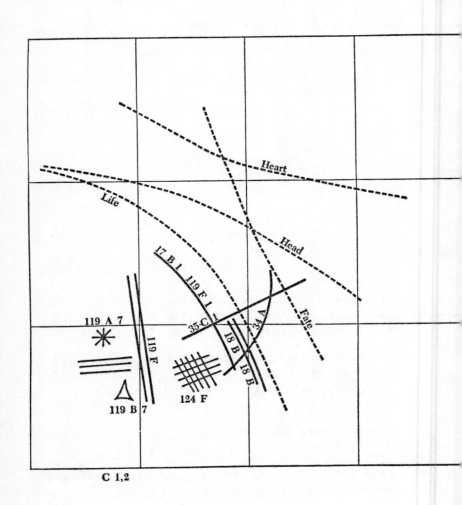

C 1,2

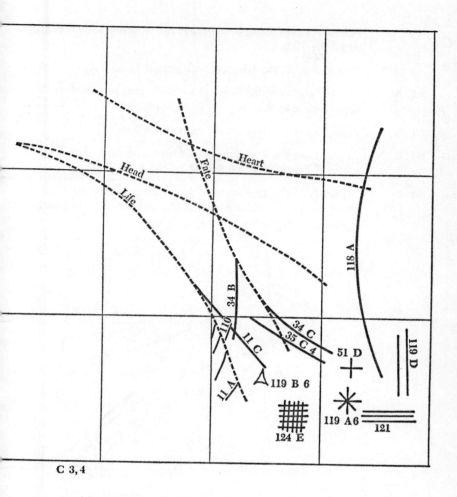

C 3,4

If a secondary line is found in Area C 4: See sections 11 C, 34 C, 35 C 4, 38 I, 51 D, 53 D, 114 D 5, 114 D 6, 118 A, 119 A 6, 119 B 5, 119 D, 121

In this area we find the notations of travel.

Travel Lines are mostly seen in hands with a *wish for travel,* since they never appear in those that are forced to travel against their will, unless they denote an *event* connected with a voyage.

All *events* pertaining to a voyage are also marked on the Life and Fate Lines.

The events marked by vertical Travel Lines are:

61 A *Travel Line running through a square* means protection from danger on a trip.

61 B *Travel Line with an island* indicates a loss of property.

61 C *Travel Line running into the Mount of Saturn* denotes a fatality, if this is also confirmed in the Life Line.

61 D *Travel Line running into the Head Line,* with a break in the Head Line at the juncture, indicates danger of illness, or head injury deriving from a voyage.

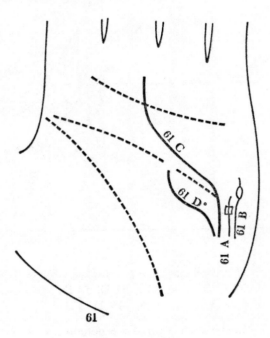

Part 2

Character Markings

Both inherited and acquired qualities can be determined by:

(1)   the shape and length of the Thumb, fingers and nails;

(2)   the shape of the hand;

(3)   the markings of the various Mounts; and

(4)   the shape and position of the lines themselves.

The abilities are shown as character markings, and the chance of success is further determined by the lines. *Character markings,* combined with *ability* and *success markings,* will determine the careers the person should follow. Comparing the character markings in the Minor and Major Hands shows whether the individual has grown away from his inherited abilities.

To determine the character of an individual by his character markings, start at section 101 and write down the characteristic that is *in italics* in each paragraph.

01   *The Thumb*

The Thumb provides the single most important indication of character. To arrive at a proper analysis, consider the combination of position, relative length and suppleness. The length of the Thumb must be seen in proportion to the fingers and entire hand.

To determine if a Thumb is long, place the hand on a flat surface and join the Thumb to the Index Finger. The Thumb reaching the second joint is considered very long. If it reaches the middle of the first phalanx it is average; and to a position below the middle of the phalanx, short.

01 A   *Position of the Thumb:* With fingers closed and Thumb spread away from the hand:

01 A 1   *Thumb close to the hand:* Denotes *dependence upon the influence of others.*

01 A 2   *Thumb wide from the hand:* Indicates *independent thinking.* The revolutionary mind has this low, wide-angled Thumb.

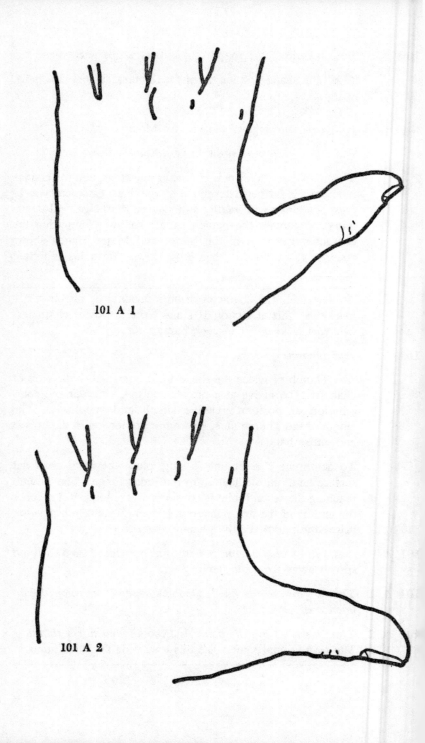

101 A 1

101 A 2

101 B *The long Thumb:* This is an indication of *power* and can be made up as follows:

101 B 1 *Long Thumb with long nail phalanx and a shorter second phalanx:* Great *power over self and others.*

101 B 1A If the long Thumb has a *long, broad, flat nail phalanx,* it denotes the *despotic* mind.

101 B 2 *Long Thumb with short nail phalanx and a long second phalanx:* Great *logic and moderate energy.*

101 B 3 *Long Thumb with equally long nail and second phalanx: Great willpower and great logic.* With properly developed lines, the mark of great leaders.

This is a very important consideration, even if the Thumb indicates great leadership, it is up to the lines in the hand to give it direction and knowledge. I have met hands that show this very strong logical Thumb but lack the properly developed Head Line to give the logic direction, or are missing the Fate or Sun Lines that spell Success.

I again must emphasize that for proper perspective—as well as where the actual results are concerned—the entire hand and its lines must be considered as a unit. To demonstrate the validity of my method, I will not tell any subject about more than one or two of the broadest and most clearly marked past events. All subsequent analysis must be done by methodically noting on paper all numbers and facts pertaining to the subject, and then eliminating any self-cancelling character traits. The actual personality will then emerge without ambiguity.

---

101 C *The short Thumb* indicates a *lack of energy, willpower and logic.* It can be combined as follows:

101 C 1 *Short Thumb with a short nail phalanx and shorter second phalanx: Lack of energy, great lack of logic.*

101 C 2 *Short Thumb with short second phalanx and shorter nail phalanx: Complete lack of willpower, lack of logic.*

101 C 3 *Short Thumb with both phalanges equally short:* This is the worst combination of lack of both willpower and logic.

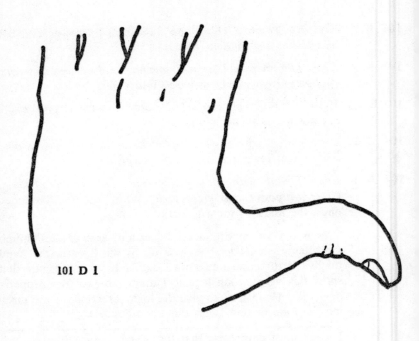

101 D 1

101 D   The *flexibility* of the Thumb is noticed by the amount of natural backward flexing which takes place when the fingers are spread far apart.

101 D 1   *The flexible Thumb:* This is the *impractical Thumb.* These individuals are easily impressed by others into extravagant spending of money and expending effort vainly.

    If this defect is combined with a long Thumb it is less damaging than with a short Thumb.

101 D 2   *The stiff Thumb:* The *practical Thumb.* This Thumb strengthens all variations encountered. From a point of view of personal achievement, the *stiff short Thumb is preferable to the medium supple* Thumb.

101 E   I have prepared the following schematic extract to find the major qualities of the various Thumb combinations in the fastest possible manner.

This section deals with close Thumb combinations; section 101 G deals with wide Thumb position.

Then each section is subdivided in flexible long, stiff long, flexible short and stiff short Thumbs. Each of the variations in relative phalanx length is then represented by a code.

By writing down the following choices

* close or wide

* flexible or stiff

* long or short

* phalanx length (relative)

the proper code can immediately be assigned. Looking up the code in sections 101 F and 101 H will describe the major traits pertaining to the subject.

Thumb combinations: schematic extract—close Thumb position

Flexible Long Thumb

Phalanx
Relative Length

1st Long
2nd Long   Code TA

1st Long
2nd Short   Code TB

1st Short
2nd Long   Code TC

1st Short
2nd Short   Code TD

Stiff Long Thumb

Phalanx
Relative Length

1st Long
2nd Long   Code TE

Flexible Short Thumb

Phalanx
Relative Length

1st Long
2nd Long   Code TI

1st Long
2nd Short   Code TJ

1st Short
2nd Long   Code TK

1st Short
2nd Short   Code TL

Stiff Short Thumb

Phalanx
Relative Length

1st Long
2nd Long   Code TM

Stiff Long Thumb		**Stiff Short Thumb**	
1st Long		1st Long	
2nd Short	Code TF	2nd Short	Code TN
1st Short		1st Short	
2nd Long	Code TG	2nd Long	Code TO
1st Short		1st Short	
2nd Short	Code TH	2nd Short	Code TP

101 F *Thumb code descriptions:*

TA *Great willpower, great logic, easily influenced, extravagant, adaptable.* Since "great logic" and "easily influenced" are mutually exclusive, this rarely seen combination denotes *a variable character,* hence this is a negative form of the characteristic "adaptable."

TB *Average energy, abundant logic, easily influenced, extravagant, adaptable—*see above. This is the normal appearance of this Thumb.

TC *Average energy, abundant logic, easily influenced by others, adaptable—*see TA for explanation of seeming contradiction of logic and the influence of others. Also note that this Thumb has less energy to resist the suggestions of others.

TD *Average energy, normal logic, easily influenced by others, adaptable.* This indicates the *good worker and manager.* The influence by others may sometimes be detrimental when this is a weak hand, indicated by short fingers and soft palm.

TE *Great willpower, great logic, adaptable.* Note that the close Thumb position, indicating dependence on others, is offset by the practical aspect of this stiff Thumb. These individuals will use only practical suggestions from others. A great *managerial* hand.

TF The same as above with the exception that it is a *less logical* hand and the dependence upon others becomes more marked.

TG *Average energy, but great logic and dependence upon others.* This Thumb formation describes the person who is not naturally energetic, but who has a very logical mind. Since he is not a lone worker, but is dependent on others with more stamina he will select his partners and surroundings with great care.

TH *Average energy, average logic, dependence on others.* This is the Thumb for *detail work.* It still is a well-developed Thumb, denoting better-than-average intelligence. With this Thumb the influence of the other fingers and lines becomes more important, since the resistance to outside thinking is just average. Good for people who work in combination with others.

TI This is the so-called *average Thumb,* without outstanding qualities. *Even workers,* not easily swayed from their original purpose but given to believe in half-truths.

TJ The Thumb of the *superstitious spendthrifts.* Their lack of logic and easily influenced character believing any tale makes the people with this Thumb the prey of the manipulator and demagogue.

TK The Thumb of the *lazy, shrewd, self-deceiving gambler.* With little logic and less willpower and an easily influenced character, the subject is his own enemy as well as others'.

TL This Thumb is *harmless.* The lack of energy, the lack of logic, and vacillation make it useless for the manipulator to steer this individual on the road to crime. These people spend their life with small, easily attained pleasures.

TM The *practical worker.* No leader, but very close to the manager and organizer. Often second in command in large organizations. Takes orders well and executes perfectly.

TN The *lack of logic* makes this Thumb less desirable as second in command by the inability to find an alternate method of executing an order. These persons would constantly refer back to the originator of the command. *Utter dependency on others*—good technicians when the orders are exceptionally clear.

TO This is the Thumb of the lower order of practical technicians. Dependent on the boss and an *automatic executor of com-*

mands. Rather *lazy* if not prodded, but handy. Can be quite shrewd if it leads to a goal without too much effort.

TP   The harmless *manual laborers,* satisfied with their lot, practical and very dependent on all their coworkers.

---

101 G   **Thumb combinations: schematic extract—wide Thumb position**

Flexible Long Thumb

Phalanx
Relative Length

1st Long
2nd Long   Code TAA

1st Long
2nd Short   Code TAB

1st Short
2nd Long   Code TAC

1st Short
2nd Short   Code TAD

Stiff Long Thumb

Phalanx
Relative Length

1st Long
2nd Long   Code TAE

1st Long
2nd Short   Code TAF

1st Short
2nd Long   Code TAG

1st Short
2nd Short   Code TAH

Flexible Short Thumb

Phalanx
Relative Length

1st Long
2nd Long   Code TAI

1st Long
2nd Short   Code TAJ

1st Short
2nd Long   Code TAK

1st Short
2nd Short   Code TAL

Stiff Short Thumb

Phalanx
Relative Length

1st Long
2nd Long   Code TAM

1st Long
2nd Short   Code TAN

1st Short
2nd Long   Code TAO

1st Short
2nd Short   Code TAP

101 H   *Thumb code descriptions*

TAA   *Great willpower, great logic, cannot be influenced by others, adaptable.* These are the born politicians, *the leaders* and guides to the behavior of others. These persons can give and take, but when a decision is made, it is forceful and logical. They sway with the political wind and will not achieve much of a technical nature. These people depend for technical information on others, which they sift out unfailingly. Good lawyers.

TAB *Great willpower, average logic, quite independent, extravagant, flexible opinions.* Still *among the leaders,* but their decisions are not always as correct as the above. The lesser politicians often have this shorter second phalanx. The independence of opinion is a great asset in such cases. They do not make very good second-position management since they are too broad in their views.

TAC *Average energy, abundant logic, independent thinking* but with theoretical rather than practical application makes this the *scientist and teacher.* This makes a good minor politician or lawyer and a major writer of fiction or textbooks.

TAD *Average energy, normal logic, independent and adaptable* make this a good *theoretical scientist.* These people are very good in their relationships with others, and they can follow a nontechnical course without erring, requiring a lot of cooperation from others.

TAE *Great willpower, great logic, adaptable, not dependent* on the decisions of others. Another *born leader.* This leader is the top inventor, research scientist, military expert or dictator. This hand can be either positive or negative in its relation to others, but is powerful in either case.

TAF *Same as above,* but *a lack of logic* makes it more probable that the power is diluted in fruitless actions.

TAG This is the Thumb of the *practical, independent, technicians,* with great logic and average energy, who do most of the practical developing of new products. Many inventors and artists have this Thumb. Musicians of this type are perfectionists in every way.

TAH The *independent, practical, average* Thumb. These people *go* *their own way* inventing minor things to make their own and others' life more pleasant. The chefs in the good restaurants do well with this thumb. Minor composers, technicians who work alone, and the perfect secretary are part of this group, as well as the top mechanics. In general they are salaried people.

TAI   *Independent small businessmen* come in this group. Of *average intelligence,* of average energy, but not too much interested in other people as coworkers put this group in self-employed, nontechnical, lesser occupations. The great adaptability of this group serves them well as accountants, minor lawyers, writers, teachers and experimental farmers.

TAJ   *Independent, adaptable, energetic, and illogical* make this the Thumb of the jack-of-all-trades who tries all angles and does not end up anywhere. The major fault of this hand is the lack of logic that pushes the person to a great number of fruitless efforts. This person will *not listen to any advice,* good or bad, and will forever try and try again. The small operator, the untalented artist and inventor come in this group.

TAK   *The lazy version of the above.*

TAL   *The harmless drifters, lazy and illogical* in their approach to life. They are not in the least interested in the opinion of others. They adapt readily to their surrounding and have a habit of blending in with it. They are not usually noticed by anyone around them.

TAM   *A very practical, independent worker.* Perfect as organizer of work and people. Can be left alone to develop minor inventions, excellent in data processing or technical work. The engineer for a large organization who is required to work independently. Here is the physician, especially the surgeon; the great musical arranger or performer.

TAN   This group of people *has to be guided constantly* by others but will work on a practical project independently for a long time. These people are dependent on their superior for layout

[104]

and planning but make good second-echelon technicians. Typical of the minor musician, draftsman, engineer.

TAO   This type Thumb marks the *independent minor technician.* Very often seen in the practical lower group of independent craftsmen, nurses, plumbers, carpenters, painters, etc. This is also the stubborn Thumb when in a generally negative hand, but then rather lazy. Shrewd, rather than active in a negative way.

TAP   This is a *lazy, illogical, independent* Thumb often seen in the *petty criminal.* At best, it is seen on the itinerant field laborer who moves from place to place.

The fingers as capability markings

After correctly cataloguing the Thumb, analyze the fingers. Each finger has a meaning in the character of the individual. Fingers indicate the *direction* the energy and logic will take. The Index Finger, for instance, will lead to politics and religion, whereas the Little Finger will lead to business and athletics. It only remains to recognize which of the fingers are the dominant ones in the hands, both Minor and Major.

It is interesting to observe the difference between both hands. This tells us something about the parents as well as the individual. Without exception, I have been able to recognize the movement away from or toward religious thought just by comparing Minor and Major Index Fingers.

So that we may recognize the features that tell us which are the dominant fingers, we have to be concerned with the following:

Relative length of the fingers compared with the length of the hand—see section 102.

Relative length of the fingers compared with each other—see section 103.

The knots between the phalanges—see section 104.

The shape of the fingertips and nails—see section 105.

The width of the closed fingertips—see section 106.

The relative length of the phalanges of the fingers—see section 107.

The position of each finger toward the other fingers—see section 108.

102 *The length of the fingers in relation to the size of the palm.*

To determine if fingers are long or short, have the subject close the fingers over the palm.

Very long fingers will reach to the wrist. Medium-long fingers reach lower Venus. Medium fingers reach middle Venus. Short fingers reach the middle of the palm.

A simple rule holds true:

102 A *Long fingers,* when compared with the palm, are *capable of minute detail,* technical and nontechnical.

102 B *Short fingers,* when compared with the palm, are *capable of broad thinking* of a general nature.

A long hand with long fingers comes under the heading of large hands, and will be discussed under hand shapes.

103 *The length of the fingers in relation to each other:* This is the most active indicator of the general type of *capability* of the subject.

The finger lengths of the Minor Hand indicate without fail the inherited capability of the subject. The Major Hand shows the actual capability.

Always first catalogue the Thumb to find the intensity of the capacities.

Schematic of relative finger lengths

* Index Finger .... Jupiter
* Middle Finger .... Saturn
* Ring Finger .... Apollo
* Little Finger .... Mercury

103 A   Compare *Jupiter and Apollo:* Apollo is longer than Jupiter. The *capability* is in the artistic rather than material world. This is one of the ways of telling the creative mind from the worldly. Note that these people can be very successful financially as well, although for them money is a secondary consideration when compared to recognition of their talent.

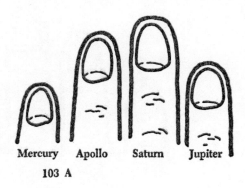

Mercury   Apollo   Saturn   Jupiter

103 A

103 B   Compare *Jupiter and Apollo:* Apollo is shorter than Jupiter.

The *capability* is in the material rather than the artistic world. This finger combination is often seen in the religious hand. The long Jupiter finger is known as an indication of formal (materialistic) religion, also seen in the hand of rulers and tyrants.

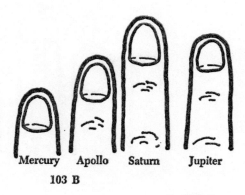

Mercury   Apollo   Saturn   Jupiter

103 B

103 C   Compare *Jupiter and Saturn:* Jupiter is as long as Saturn, both are longer than Apollo.

This is an unusual combination seen in the hand of *extreme egotists.* The material results condone every honest and dishonest action. Very often self-destructive, since it creates many enemies.

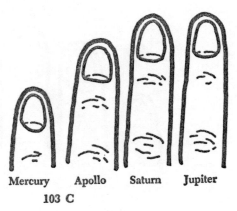

Mercury   Apollo   Saturn   Jupiter

103 C

103 D   Compare *Apollo and Mercury:* Mercury is almost as long as Apollo, both are shorter than Jupiter.

This is the hand of *the public speaker, the expressive philosopher.* This long Little Finger helps an underdeveloped Thumb and indicates the abstract scientist. This is a rare combination.

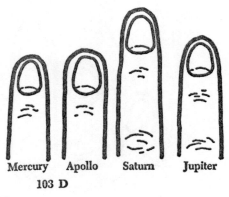

Mercury   Apollo   Saturn   Jupiter

103 D

103 E   Compare *Saturn and Apollo:* Apollo is as long as Saturn, both are longer than Jupiter.

This denotes a combination of artistic with fatalistic trends. The real gambler, not only with property but with life itself.

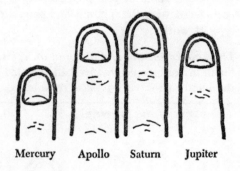

Mercury   Apollo   Saturn   Jupiter

103 E

104   *Knotted fingers:* The knot between the first and second phalanx (between the nail phalanx and the middle phalanx of the fingers) is known as the knot of *mental order,* the second knot is the knot of *material order.*

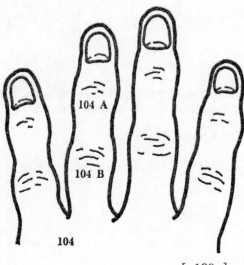

104

104 A   *The knot of mental order:* When this knot is seen on all fingers in varying degrees it indicates that the person can *think* in an *organized* and detailed manner.

104 B   *The knot of material order:* This knot is seen on all people who are capable of *fine physical work*. The knot has to be considered with the Thumb and fingertips to determine the type of work.

104 C   *The knot of mental and material order:* This is the best combination for people involved in detailed operations. This is the hand of the *very precise technician*.

---

105   *The shape of the fingertips*

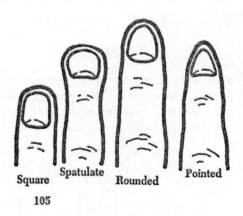

Square   Spatulate   Rounded   Pointed

105

The shape of the fingertips is the main indication of the type of capability we are dealing with.

The various shapes are:

* Square .... A

* Spatulate .... B

* Rounded C

* Pointed .... D

Each finger may have any one of the above tips, each with its own indication, depending upon the finger that is involved.

The general rule pertaining to the fingertip shape tells us that the *square ending* means that the elementary form of that finger dominates; the *spatulate ending* means that the practical form of that finger dominates; the *rounded ending* means that the mental qualities of the finger become important; and the *pointed ending* imparts totally psychic qualities.

105 A   *Square fingers*

105 A 1   *Index Finger square:* This is the elementary form. Orderly, practical, moderately religious, strong-willed. *Dogmatic* and inflexible. Lower-echelon military men and women.

105 A 2   *Middle Finger square:* This is the elementary form. *Gloomy,* cynical, practical in a small way. In a bad hand a miser, in a good hand an economist. Cautious.

105 A 3   *Ring Finger square:* The elementary form. The practical minor artist. *Minor appreciation of culture* in general.

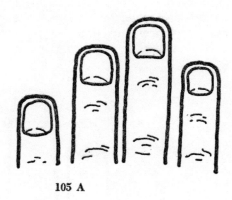

105 A

105 A 4   *Little Finger square:* The elementary form. The practical minor businessman or woman. Minor athlete, *restless.*

105 B *Spatulate fingers*

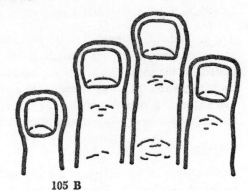

105 B

105 B 1 *Index Finger spatulate:* This is the independent form. The independent religious worker, also the crank. *Materialistic,* practical about social problems—law-enforcement officer.

105 B 2 *Middle Finger spatulate:* This is the practical form. Cynical, cautious and precise. This person takes and executes orders with great precision. The practical criminologist often has this form of Middle Finger.

105 B 3 *Ring Finger spatulate:* The *practical artist.* Musician, performer. Appreciation of art.

105 B 4 *Little Finger spatulate:* The practical *business executive.* The stage performer, practical lawyer, minor scientist, minor medical studies.

105 C *Rounded fingers*

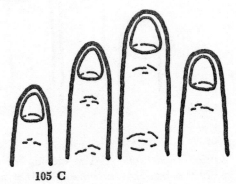

105 C

105 C 1 *Index Finger rounded:* The form between the pure thinker and the practical worker. The religious mystic, the active *searcher for truth* and unknown powers, the hand seen in Eastern cultures. Impulsive and charitable.

105 C 2 *Middle Finger rounded:* Capable caution makes this a fine administrator. The basic disbelief and mistrust of others puts this hand in strong *critical* positions. The upper-echelon watchdog. Extremely *cautious* and precise. Unsocial but a great believer in predestination and the occult.

105 C 3 *Ring Finger rounded:* The active composer, the better painter, general appreciation of art and people. This form works well with others and is usually well appreciated.

This is the *most successful form of creative finger* from a personal point of view. A practical designer, the architect-designer, the best performing musicians come in this category. Note that writers do not necessarily fall in this category; only writers on the arts will.

105 C 4 *Little Finger rounded:* Top-level business executives fall in this category. Great sense for science as applied to business, for law and politics, excellent students of medicine and practical mathematics, including the most outstanding dramatic artists. The *practical scientific mind* can be powerful in the negative sense also: great swindlers and cheats in a bad hand (see section 112).

105 D *Pointed fingers:* The pointed finger carries the hand into the realm of the purely mental.

105 D 1 *Index Finger pointed:* This form withdraws from the world in a contemplation of life. The Yogi and the psychic are examples of this type. All is in the mind: They are so sensitive that they are melancholy. *Full of emotion,* insensitive to most baser material things. They will think, rarely write, about the universe, and are very hard to get to express an opinion. The impractical far outreaches the practical.

[113]

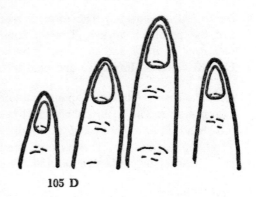

105 D

105 D 2 *Middle Finger pointed:* This makes a *withdrawn person,* completely emotional and cynical. Some great composers have this finger shape, but their music is tragic. Not good for business, extreme *isolationist* and quite fatalistic.

105 D 3 *Ring Finger pointed:* The finger of the composer, the top theoretical philosopher, the idealist. Quite impractical, but the ideas are solid. Very trusting and excellent when working together with the owner of the rounded or spatulate Ring Finger. People with these fingers have much trouble in everyday life, and they will automatically follow any seemingly strong guidance. The psychic hand has this type of pointed-finger ending. Extremely sensitive and easily damaged emotionally. *Originator of abstract ideas.*

105 D 4 *Little Finger pointed:* This is the mark of the most expressive actor, the political theorist, also the most accomplished crook and cheat. This is also the theoretical, *abstract scientific mind,* the inventor.

105 E   Fingertip combinations: schematic extract

	Jupiter (Index)	Saturn (Middle)
Square	dogmatic	gloomy
Spatulate	materialist	executes orders
Rounded	searcher for truth	cautious, critical
Pointed	full of emotion	withdrawn, isolationist

	Apollo (Ring)	**Mercury (Little)**
Square	art appreciation	restless
Spatulate	practical artist	business executive
Rounded	creative success	practical scientist
Pointed	abstract idealist	abstract scientist

105 F   *The shape of the nails:*

As we have seen in section 50, the nails indicate health and attendant problems. Since health and temperament seem to be connected, we can expect and find certain nail types to correspond to emotional characteristics.

105 F 1   *Long nails:* The narrow long nail belongs to the psychic hand. We find these people to be quite calm, even-tempered and resigned to their fate. When the rest of the hand is not typical of the psychic character, we are dealing with disease.

The wide and long nail is normal on the philosophic hand and is typical for a well-informed, understanding person.

105 F 2   *Short nails:* Short-nailed people, like those with short fingers, are broad in their understanding but highly critical of others. Since they grasp most facts at a glance and are usually impatient, they are occasionally quite violent toward those who lack their analytical mind.

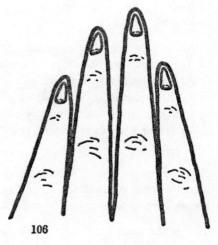

106

106 *The width of the closed fingertips,* compared with the base of the fingers.

106 A *Tapering of the fingertips:* This is a comparison between the so-called mental world and the practical world. In general, tapering of the fingers to the tips emphasizes thought over practicality.

106 A 1 *Tapering with short fingers:* This is the *balanced hand.* It is slightly more elementary than intuitive and practical in a broad sense. Good for marketing and commercial lower-echelon work.

106 A 2 *Tapering with long fingers:* Much more *precise* than above. Can be a typical expert in a narrower area. The mark of the marketing analyst.

106 B *No tapering of the fingertips:* This is seen in the so-called square hand and emphasizes the practical over the mental. This is the *no-nonsense* hand.

106 B 1 *No tapering—short fingers:* The practical, unimaginative hand. These people do well but follow instructions, both good and bad. *Impulsive.*

106 B 2 *No tapering—long fingers:* The *practical, imaginative* hand. Can do very detailed, exact manual and creative work. Quite fastidious.

106 C *Extreme tapering:* The extremely tapered hand is the hand of the purely emotional person who is driven away from reality by the overly sensitive nature of the very slim fingertips. These people at best *function poorly in our society;* they fear much, which exists mainly in their imagination. Normally found with short fingers, reinforcing the lack of exactness and logic.

106 C 1 *Extreme tapering with short, stubby fingers:* This is actually a combination of short fingers and heavy third phalanges, denoting a *low-grade mentality* and a lack of thoughtfulness.

This is the complete form of *self-indulgence.*

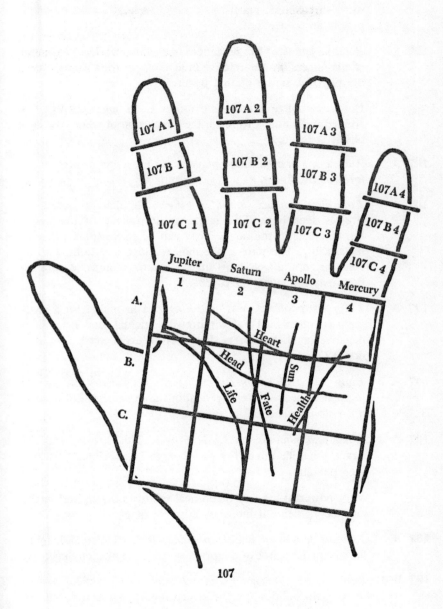

107 A 1
107 B 1
107 C 1
107 A 2
107 B 2
107 C 2
107 A 3
107 B 3
107 C 3
107 A 4
107 B 4
107 C 4

Jupiter   Saturn   Apollo   Mercury

A.   1   2   3   4

B.

C.

Heart

Head

Life   Fate   Sun   Health

The completely materialistic mentality, often combined with some shrewdness, make this a negative hand as far as other people are concerned.

107 *Relative length of the phalanges of the fingers:* The phalanges of the fingers are the relative indications of the mental versus the physical nature of that finger.

Here a complete mixture is possible. Each finger must be examined individually to reach the conclusion of where the emphasis is located.

107 A Rule: *Long first (or nail) phalanx is the mental or theoretical form* of the finger.

107 A 1 *Long first phalanx on Index Finger:* Emphasizes emotions, stresses sensitivity. This is the most psychic of the finger forms. All is in the mind. They can be so sensitive as to be melancholy. The pure spokesman for love and faith. *Full of emotion,* not affected by material surroundings, except as they may influence the psyche.

107 A 2 *Long first phalanx on Middle Finger:* This makes for a *complete isolationist.* Total withdrawal, suicidal tendencies in a negative hand. Suicide is shown as an event mark (see section 12 E 4).

107 A 3 *Long first phalanx on Ring Finger:* This stresses the mental in creative people. We now deal in the extreme with the seer, *the visionary* and the medium.

107 A 4 *Long first phalanx on Little Finger:* This stresses the abstract, scientific mind. *Far-out thought* is associated with this long phalanx.

Very powerful for any theoretical mathematician, and in the case of medicine it indicates intuitive diagnosis.

107 B *Relative length of middle phalanx:* Rule: The middle phalanx is the indicator of the practical strength of each finger.

107 B 1 *Long middle phalanx in Index Finger:* The practical worker in religion, politics and the armed forces. No leader, but not a selfish operator. Often seen in uniform. *Generally a servant of the people.*

107 B 2   *Long middle phalanx in Middle Finger:* A good and efficient lone worker. Very cautious and practical with money. Does not easily achieve riches, but saves well. *Practical critic,* in all fields.

107 B 3   *Long middle phalanx in Ring Finger:* The *appreciation of useful beauty* make this the mark of the decorator, designer, practical musical performer. For this group, achieving is the main goal and money is a secondary consideration.

107 B 4   *Long middle phalanx in Little Finger: The practical worker in the sciences and business.* The stress is on the attainable goal in business, the state of the art in medicine, the "now" in science. These people make the best possible use of the tools of science at their disposal. They do not originate revolutionary ideas, but know where to find things they need to conduct their affairs successfully. Their negative side is quite powerful, and they are among the best organizers of crime.

107 C   Rule: *Long third phalanx is the physical, worldly form of the finger.*

107 C 1   *Long third phalanx on Index Finger:* Emphasis on the worldly in religion, pride and autocracy. *Dogmatic and commercial* in money matters. Inflexible and a showy dresser. Career soldier, money-oriented politician. When both wide and long, self-indulgent: a *gourmand.*

107 C 2   *Long third phalanx on Middle Finger:* The *miser.* Hoards property and mistrusts others completely. When his phalanx is both wide and long, a recluse and misanthrope.

107 C 3   *Long third phalanx on the Ring Finger:* The emphasis is on *personal luxury.* This is the mark of the flashy-looking artist. No taste, but plenty of show. It marks the mixed-up dabbler in the "arts."

107 C 4   *Long third phalanx on the Little Finger:* The worldly aspect of business is emphasized. Pseudo scientific, very restless, *erratic*. The fraud, the charlatan in negative hands.

108   *The position of the fingers relating to each other:* The fingers can be set equidistant from each other at the base, they can be turned toward each other, and they can be straight on the hand.

108 A   With fingers spread apart, the *Index and Middle Fingers are wide apart* at the base: This separates the personality traits of Jupiter from the worldly traits of Saturn. It usually also separates the Mounts (see section 110) under these fingers which indicates the same: *It reinforces the independent characteristic.* With a low-set, wide-angled Thumb and a strong first phalanx of the Thumb, we get the isolationist, anarchist, lone revolutionary.

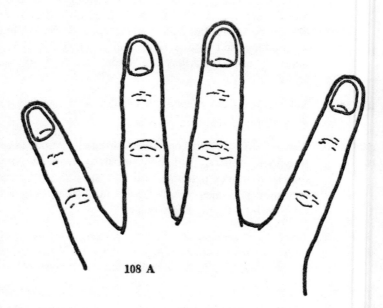

108 A

108 B   With fingers spread apart, *the Ring and Little Fingers are wide apart at the base:* This separates the artistic and business aspects of the hand. It makes the *actions independent.* In the extreme case, this is an active revolutionary.

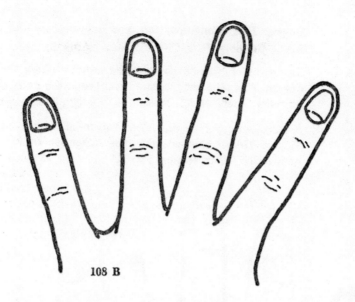

108 B

108 C *The fingertips leaning toward each other:* From the leaning of the fingertips a position can be found where the emphasis of the hand is located.

108 C 1 *Fingertips emphasize the position of Jupiter—*all lean to the Index Finger: This strengthens the characteristics of Jupiter, described in section 110 A.

108 C 2 *Fingertips emphasize the position between Index and Middle Finger:* A balance between the fatalistic and sensitive worldly emotions. This reduces the gloomy tendencies that the Middle Finger emphasizes, but it also reduces the leadership qualities of the Index Finger.

108 C 3 *Fingertips emphasize the Middle Finger—*all lean to the Middle Finger: This strengthens the type indication of the Saturnian described in section 110 B.

108 C 4 *Fingertips emphasize the position between Middle and Ring Fingers:* This weakens the type description of both Saturn and Apollo.

108 C 5 *Fingertips emphasize the Ring Finger—*all lean to the Ring

Finger: This strengthens the type indication of the Apollonian, described in section 110 C.

108 C 6 *Fingertips emphasize the position between Ring and Little Finger:* This weakens the type description of both Apollo and Mercury.

108 C 7 *Fingertips emphasize the Little Finger*—all lean to the Little Finger: This strengthens the type indication of the Mercurian, described in section 110 D.

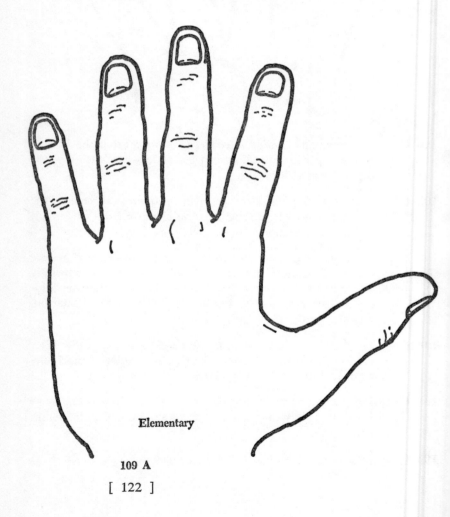

Elementary

109 A

[122]

108 C 8   *Fingertips pointing straight up:* The hand is balanced and none of the traits are emphasized by the fingertip position. All information is obtained from the fingers themselves (see sections 105 and 106).

109   *The shape of the hand:* In general, the *large* hand is capable of *minute detail,* the *small* hand shows *broad and organizational thinking.*

109 A   When the palm is *thick and short,* with short fingers, we are dealing with the *elementary type.* Secondary characteristics

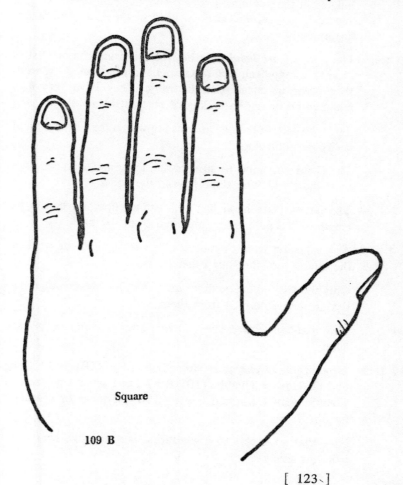

Square

109 B

of the elementary type are a *short and thick Thumb* and very few lines in the hand. This hand belongs to the most primitive element of the population. A lack of mental capacity is immediately evident. If the Thumb shows a large first phalanx (excessive willpower), the subject is capable of very destructive action through low instinctive drives.

109 B   *The square hand:* The square hand, with *finger width about equal to the palm,* is the *practical hand.* The square hand is as wide at the wrist as at the base of the fingers, without bulging at the percussion. The secondary characteristic is the square fingertips, well-defined lines in the palm and square fingernails.

109 C   The *pure square hand* indicates the following characteristics: orderly, methodical, *well organized* and practical. As a group they favor practical scientific work. They have *very little imagination* or understanding of abstract ideas.

To make certain that we are dealing with a pure square hand, verify the following:

The Head Line must be straight and long; under no condition must the Head Line slope toward the wrist.

The pure square hand has square fingertips and fingers the length of the palm when observed from the back.

Any variation from this norm either strengthens or weakens the qualities of the square hand.

Only the reinforcing qualities are given; the weakening qualities are easily derived from them.

109 D   *The modified square hand—factors strengthening the square hand:*

109 D 1   *Organizational character* strengthened by: (101 B 1) Long first phalanx of Thumb; (101 B 2) Long second phalanx of Thumb; (104) Knotted fingers; (105) Square or spatulate fingertips.

Note that an excess of organization is a negative characteristic, the crank.

109 D 2 *Logic strengthened by:* Long second phalanx of Thumb (101 B 2), long fingers. A good hand for the practical scientist.

109 D 3 *Lack of imagination offset by mixed fingertips:* This adds imagination, but in many varied areas. This hand has many practical ideas but does little about any one of them. A *tinkerer.*

Also offset by a Head Line sloping toward Luna.

109 E *The tapered hand:* This is a hand with the finger base slightly narrower than the base of the palm, near the wrist.

The tapered hand is normally seen with *spatulate fingertips,* and the fingers are the length of the palm when viewed from the back.

109 E 1 The *pure tapered* hand: Restless, energetic, loves action, *continually looking for new methods* and places. Original in their approach even in everyday functions. Rube Goldberg types. In the negative form, a nuisance to others for the same reasons.

109 E 2 *The inverse tapered hand:* This is the same as 109 E 1, but the taper is at the wrist and the finger base is wider than the wrist. The characteristics of the *inverse* tapered hand are *similar to the tapered hand,* but energy is expended on *more practical, worldly efforts.*

With this hand the new approaches are much more practical, and direct. This type is actually a modification between the square and tapered hand.

109 F *The narrow or philosophic hand:* This is a narrow hand, with long fingers and *well-developed knots* in the fingers. Fingertips are normally rounded.

The narrow hand is the impractical hand, the long fingers are the sign of great detail and the knots denote a great sense of order. The round fingertip is a sign of activity.

The combination carries the subject into the mental world, away from the practical; out of the mechanized society, into the active analysis of thought: for example, the active student of archeology, the Bible analyst, the student of the Occult.

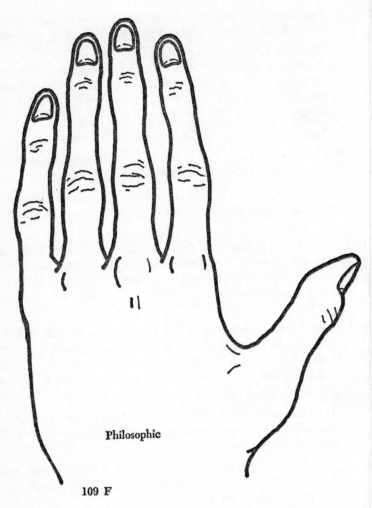

Philosophic

109 F

109 F 1 *The pure philosophic hand:* Studious, *contemplative,* loving the beautiful, the mystery of things. No interest in worldly values. Very quiet and set apart from most other people; mostly self-centered and proud.

The negative connotation of this hand is that it does not fit easily into the worldly scheme of things. The subject has trouble earning a living.

109 G   *The psychic or totally mental hand:* The pure psychic hand
is a narrow hand like the philosophic hand, but with tapering, very long fingers. The order knots are absent and the
fingers pointed.

The narrowness of the hand precludes a practical nature; the
long fingers give love of detail; the pointed long first phalanx
carries the hand into the purely mental.

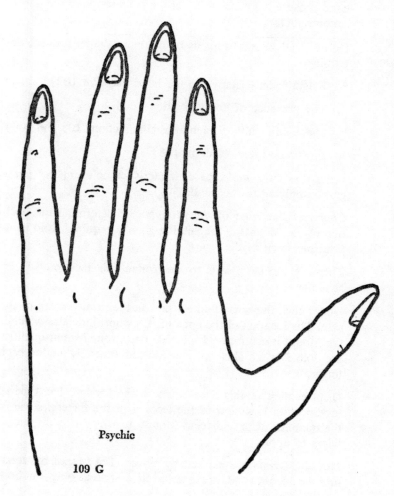

Psychic

109 G

When the line of intuition is added to this combination, we have the medium; without that, *the visionary idealist.* This type loves the beautiful, trusts in the world and fate and lives on a very high emotional and mental plane. Their sense of religion or life is purely spiritual. They love mysticism but are not usually engaged in any activity connected with it.

109 H   *The mixed hand:* A square palm is not normally found with knotted long pointed fingers. This is an example of a mixed hand because the relationship of the palm shape to the fingers is contradictory.

Do not analyze mixed hands by the hand shape. Instead, determine:

* Finger length relative to the hand (section 102)

* The presence of knots (section 104)

* Shape and width of each fingertip (sections 105 and 106)

* Finger positions (section 108)

Write down the *italicized* characteristics of each, per paragraph applying to the hand.

110   *Character markings of the Mounts:* To determine the position of the Mounts, a magnifying glass is required if no hand print has been made.

There is an easy way to determine the location of the Mounts:

Under each finger we find a whorl in the print pattern of the skin. The location of the apex of this whorl indicates whether the Mount is central or displaced. The strong Mount qualities are found when this apex is located centrally under each finger.

Displacement of this apex weakens the Mount. The type of modification is similar to the leaning of the fingers: some of the qualities of the adjacent Mount, to which it is displaced, begin to apply.

Not all Mounts are marked by apices. The Mount of Venus and the Mount of Mars are descriptive of areas only, but both

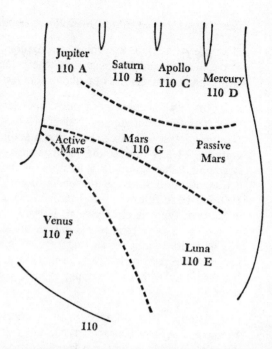

are of great importance in reference to the character and sometimes event markings in the hand lines.

Our main interest is in the *area* in the hand, described by the Mount's *name,* and the *strength* which the central or strongly developed Mount adds to the character.

Proper locating of the Mount is necessary for understanding the smooth crossing event lines of the Life Line described in section 12. Each of the Mounts is used topographically as well as to indicate a characteristic.

All Mounts are important to the topographical palmist since the lines from and to these areas have exact meanings, depending on the Mount description of that area. These meanings are described in the section on shapes and position of lines (section 111).

Type codes for character markings: There are a group of markings that are particular to a type of character.

These types are separated in seven main divisions:

The pure Jupiterian, Saturnian, Apollonian, Mercurian, Martian, Lunarian and Venusian take their names from the area in the hand that stands out above the rest.

I have rarely encountered a pure type demonstrating all the characteristics belonging exclusively to that division. The beginning analyst will often think that a subject is a pure representative of any one of the main groups, but as experience is gained (after studying a number of hands and especially if the routine outlined at the beginning of Part Two, section 100, has been followed) and the character traits emerge, the mixture of types is clearly seen. However, a person does not have to be a pure type to exhibit an unusually high percentage of traits belonging to that type. When I start to see a very definite pattern in the type markings, I will assume that I am dealing with such a type, even if not all of the details seem to correspond.

For instance, if I am faced with a compromise between a Venus and Apollo character type, and I deal with the subject directly—in other words, not from a print—and I observe that the eyes are very weak, then I immediately will favor the Apollo side of the choice. Venus is not known for weak eyes. There are also ways of finding the emphasis from the lines in the hand, which are described separately.

110 A   *The Mount of Jupiter:* Located under the Index Finger. If the skin whorl is located centrally under the finger, the Jupiterian characteristics become more pronounced.

The area description is *religion* and *leadership*.

The *Jupiterian* is recognized by: Index Finger (Jupiter) longer than Ring Finger (Apollo). Mount of Jupiter central and well developed.

There are a few typically Jupiterian personal characteristics. Their leaning is toward the church as an organization, toward the army (again as an organization), politics and anything with order and law in general. Also, in some contrast, they love nature. When I meet a person who exudes the love of great order, I immediately expect the Jupiterian hand.

110 B   *The Mount of Saturn:* Located under the Middle Finger. If the skin whorl is located centrally under the finger, the Saturnian characteristics become more pronounced. The area description is *pessimism* and *bone troubles.*

The *Saturnian* is recognized by: Middle Finger (Saturn) flanked by Index and Ring Fingers of *equal length,* both short. Small Little Finger. Mount of Saturn central and well developed.

In varying degrees, depending on purity of type, the Saturnian is gloomy, fastidious or just plain critical. The ending of the middle fingertip and the length of the three phalanges will show in which category the Saturnian under observation falls. To meet Saturnians is like meeting critics: They just do not approve of anything out of the ordinary and are never overjoyed at having their palms analyzed!

This is a *long, tall person.* The very length and thinness make this an easily detected type.

110 C   *The Mount of Apollo:* Located under the Ring Finger. If the skin whorl is located centrally under the finger, the Apollonian characteristics become more pronounced.

The area description is *art* and *eyes.*

The *Apollonian* is recognized by: Ring Finger (Apollo) longer than Index Finger. Mount of Apollo central and well developed. These people often have weak eyes, which will help identification.

The Apollonians are optimists. They love art, but do not perform or create works of art unless they are of the purer type, with strong Sun Lines and positive markings on the Mount of Apollo.

Their basic weakness is that they befriend people rather indiscriminately, and suffer the consequences.

110 D   *The Mount of Mercury:* Located under the Little Finger. If the skin whorl is located centrally under the finger, the Mercurian characteristics become more pronounced. The area description is *travel* and *business*.

The *Mercurian* is recognized by: Little Finger (Mercury) long in comparison. Mount of Mercury central and well developed. These are very restless, active people.

Mercury, the god of merchants and thieves, has given his name to the type of people who fall in this category. The Mercurian is shrewd in varying degrees, again depending on purity of type, often a lawyer, and also the most active type physically. To differentiate between the Apollonian and the Mercurian, we only have to compare the patience of both. Apollo loves to sit and observe; Mercury will jump and hop and act. Mercurians are outstanding athletes. With vertical lines marked on the Mount they are capable of scientific studies and are most successful as physicians and scientists. The negative form of Mercurian is the super confidence man and crook.

110 E   *The Mount of Luna:* Located at the percussion toward the wrist. There are no skin whorls associated with this Mount.

The area description is a *wandering mind* and *water*.

The *Lunarian* is recognized by: A bulge in the area of Luna: the side of the hand bulges at the wrist and the Mount is highly developed (rare). The round face with low forehead is an easy recognition mark.

The Lunarians are a strange type. Depending on the purity of the characteristics, they approach insanity. Their imagination is extreme and their borderline between rational and irrational is easily crossed. The purer type is fortunately not often encountered, but under any form of pressure any Lunarian will become restless. If the hand-line analyst suspects a Lunarian of the purer type, the reading should be done very lightly since they are very superstitious and may start to imagine terrible things at once. They are very often extremely artistic and creative; in fact, they number among themselves some of the greatest composers and painters as well as writers.

[132]

110 E 1 *The Mount of Luna well developed:* This indicates mental and emotional restlessness. A great wish to travel or see and do new things is typical.

110 E 2 *The Mount of Luna overdeveloped:* Here we are dealing with the Lunarian type. The Mount now dominates the hand. The emotional and physical restlessness becomes a liability if not checked.

In the best cases the Lunarian type, with the strong outward and upward bulge of this Mount, are romantic and imaginative writers and thinkers; at its worst we are dealing with the lunatic. The Head Line as a character mark will tell the difference (see sections 114 B 3, 4).

The excessive wish for change makes this overdeveloped Mount the mark of the failure in business, since not any single venture will satisfy the errant mind.

The typical Lunarian reacts physically and emotionally to water.

110 E 3 *The Mount of Luna underdeveloped:* This indicates a lack of imagination and is not the mark of the Lunarian.

110 F *The Mount of Venus:* Located at the base of the Thumb. There are no skin whorls associated with this Mount.

The area description is *sex and love.*

The *Venusian* is recognized by: A far-into-the-hand sweeping Life Line that makes the area of Venus bulge.

The Venusian is a graceful person, a charming type, unusually attractive to the opposite sex, from which many of their problems stem. They love their family, they love music, are very cheerful but often lack the strong Thumb and Head Line to guide them. As a pure type they need much help from others and are often unlucky in their choice of partners in marriage. The inferior type of Venusian is interested in sex on a simpler scale and sells itself for that purpose.

110 F 1 *The Mount of Venus well developed:* This is the mark of the healthy hand with a normal sex drive.

The Mount describes all matters involving the family. Lines originating on this Mount show the relationship of the subject toward the family and affections.

The typical Venusian is best described as an affectionate person, with a great desire for beauty in things and people, generous and with a joy for life. Very sensitive to music, without necessarily performing. The normal well-developed Mount sweeps wide into the hand and is bordered by the Life Line.

110 F 2   *The Mount of Venus overdeveloped:* This indicates an excessive sex drive and violent passions if the Thumb shows excessive willpower at the same time.

110 F 3   *The Mount of Venus underdeveloped:* Indication of a lack of sex drive and a general lack of Venusian characteristics.

The simplest way in which to assert if there is a lack of development in the Mount is to observe the sweep of the Life Line into the hand. When the Life Line runs straight along the middle of the palm, there is a possible lack of development of the area. We deal with a well-developed Mount when the Life Line sweeps far into the palm, especially when it rounds toward the Head Line.

110 G   *The areas of Mars:* The areas, sometimes referred to as the upper and lower Mounts of Mars, are hard to separate in most hands. As a rule it is best to consider the entire palm of the hand, under the Finger Mounts of Jupiter, Saturn, Apollo and Mercury and above the Mounts of Venus and Luna, as the areas of Mars.

The area of Mars under Jupiter denotes the active Mars type. The area of Mars under Mercury is the passive Mars type.

The character of Mars is described best by either the terms aggressive or resistant, depending on which Mount is the dominating one, the area of Mars under Jupiter gives the aggressor, the Mercury Mars type resists attack.

The area description is *mechanical* and *war*. The Martian is recognized by:

A bulge in the area of Mars—the side of the hand bulges out under the Little Finger, but not at the wrist.

These people are either very aggressive or defensive.

Red hair is one of the characteristics of the pure Martian.

Martians think in terms of aggression or defense. They show extreme skill in the manipulation of people in times of stress, and they exhibit unusual courage or ignorance of danger. They often seem foolhardy and reckless, but as a type they get away with more dangerous situations than any of the other types. They are made for war, but know how to avoid risks better than any other type. A typical example was a rather pure Martian, with red hair and all the other attributes, who when already far advanced in age, avoided being killed by a taxi on a streetcorner by jumping six feet out of the path of the oncoming vehicle.

111 *The shape and position of the lines as character markings*

The lines in the hand have been described as event markings in the first part of this book.

The lines perform two other very important functions: *They describe the character* of the person by the route that they take through the palm. They add the *explanation to an event line* by their source and ending.

All lines that serve as character markings can be found in so-called good or strong hands and bad or weak hands.

112 *Good and bad hands defined*

A good hand stresses the *positive* qualities of the Mounts and lines of the hand, a bad hand the *negative* ones.

It must be realized that a line can be negative but not bad. For instance, for a person who is interested in geology, a mathematician's Head Line could be considered negative. But the line itself is not a bad line. Similar examples are constantly encountered, and the term "bad hands" is mainly derived from the effect which people with these hands have on others.

112 A   The main *positive* marks are:

A strong Thumb, first and second phalanges long, willpower and logic developed. Wide from the hand: independent (section 101).

A hard hand, stressing the practical form of hand.

Long fingers for detailed work (section 102).

Short fingers for broad decision (section 102).

Clearly marked, unbroken lines of Life, Head and Heart.

Absence of Health Line for good health (section 40).

Absence of grilles on any Mount (section 124).

112 B   The main *negative marks* are:

A weak Thumb, no logic, no willpower (section 101).

A soft flabby hand, no energy.

Short fingers for lack of mentality (section 102).

Long fingers for exaggerated preciseness (section 102).

Chained, laddered or otherwise deformed broken lines of Life, Head and Heart.

Poorly marked, twisted Health Line (section 42).

Grilles, bars, crosslines on any Mount (section 52).

113   *The Life Line as character marking:* The Life Line is not the most important indicator of character, since it is the key line to *events* that have happened and are potentially in the offing. It is only important in two ways: in the limit it puts upon the area of Venus, and in the health prognosis as it affects the mood and character of people.

A healthy mind in a healthy body is verified by the Life and Head Lines.

113 A   The Life Line can indicate the character by its sweep through the palm, wide into the hand, down to the wrist: This makes the Mount of Venus very large, it indicates physical strength and *good health.*

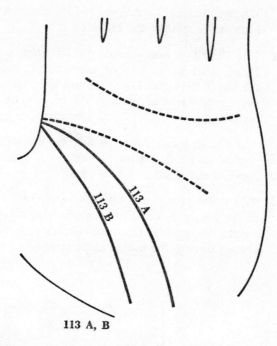

113 A, B

If the line is clear and distinct without breaks, it indicates a good, long life. It also gives a very *positive outlook on life*.

113 B　The Life Line sweeps down, close to the Thumb: This indicates delicate health and consequently a quieter nature. It produces a *withdrawn character*.

114　*The Head Line as character marking:* The Head Line is the main indicator for the mental capacity of the subject.

As an event marking it has been discussed in section 19 and up. We now observe the various meanings of the areas through which the Head Line sweeps.

Read only Major Hand markings for the subject.

114 A　*The origin of the Head Line:* The Head Line starts at a point under Jupiter, but just above Mars.

This is the normal starting point for a Head Line.

We now consider how close the Life Line comes to the Head Line at the start of the Head Line.

114 A 1   *The Head Line touches the Life Line at the start* in the Major Hand: This is the sign of the *cautious mind.* The longer the Head Line and Life Line run together at the start, the stronger the fear of venture will be. This is the sign of the timid.

There is an important point to note: the above is not an inherited trait if the Minor Hand has a spacing at the start, between the Head and Life Line.

114 A 2   *The Head Line is separated from the Life Line at the start* in the Major Hand: Note the width of the separation. The separation indicates the *independence of the mind:* the wider the separation, the more independence.

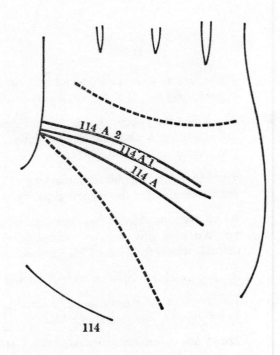

114

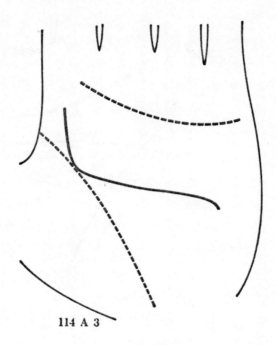

114 A 3

If the separation becomes very large, the mentality is typical of the foolhardy and careless (see also below).

114 A 3 *The Head Line starts under Jupiter widely separated from the Life Line* but joins it at a later position. This is a so-called Jupiter Head Line: The origin on the Mount of Jupiter indicates *brilliance,* but it joins the Life Line. Instead of a reckless disregard for Life, it becomes tempered by this joining and is the most brilliant starting mark for the Head Line, capable of controlling others and making the best decisions.

With this mark, make sure that the Head Line is long and remains in the areas of Mars for maximum worldly achievement (section 110 G).

114 A 4 *The Head Line starts inside the Life Line* in the areas between Venus and Mars: We now deal with the aggressive nature of Mars combined with excessive caution and attendant

[139]

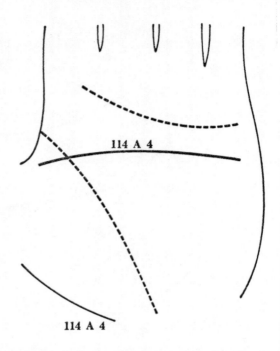

114 A 4

114 A 4

worry. This is the minor *persecution complex,* the so-called Martian Head Line.

This has the exact opposite meaning as the Jupiter Head Line, and consequently it is not a good sign in the relationship with other people, who will all be regarded with mistrust.

114 B *The course of the Head Line through the palm:* The Head Line separates people into two groups, one with an aptitude for mathematics and the other with a bent for languages. All variations between these types are shown by the course which the Head Line follows through the palm. It is necessary to know which Head Line normally belongs to which hand type to evaluate the intensity of meaning, but it takes very little routine to be able to spot the difference. This is explained in section 114 H.

114 B 1 *The Head Line sweeps straight across the hand,* staying in the area of Mars: This is the practical Head Line. This Head

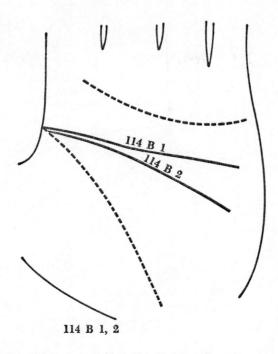

114 B 1, 2

Line always corresponds to the mind known as *mathematical,* or practical.

It is also the commonsense Head Line and does not denote much imagination.

114 B 2 *The Head Line has a very slight slope along its length:* This sloping is very significant. The slope is now toward the area of Luna, the area of the imagination.

Whenever the Head Line starts to bend down, we find a change away from the practical, mathematical toward the theoretical, imaginative type of hand.

114 B 3 *The Head Line slopes considerably toward Luna,* from the middle of the hand: This is the *perfect balance* of the average hand. It means that the influence of Luna, the imagination, makes itself felt at the same time that the practical side of the individual is evident. The imagination develops at a later

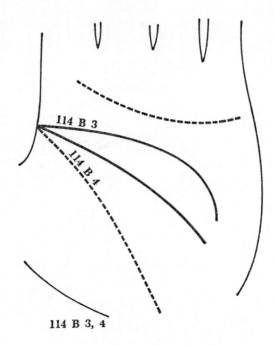

114 B 3, 4

time, depending upon the age on the Head Line indicated by the start of the sloping.

114 B 4 *The Head Line slopes toward Luna,* from the start: This is the mark of the *imaginative hand.* The more the slope, the more the imagination is developed and the less the practical side can be used.

The imagination is used according to the type of hand: in religion (Jupiter), morbidity (Saturn), in the arts (Apollo), in invention and business (Mercury), in war (Mars), in fiction writing (Luna), in sex and love (Venus). See section 110 for type description.

114 C *Termination of the Head Line*

114 C 1 *The Head Line terminates* very close to its start *under Saturn:* This is a sure sign of *early death* due to mental disorder when it appears in the Major Hand. See event marks in section 24.

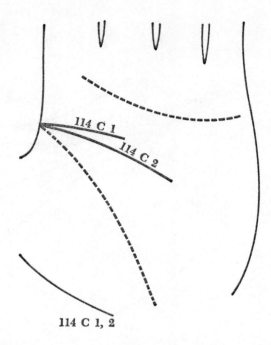

114 C 1, 2

114 C 2 *The Head Line terminates before the middle palm:* This is the sign of the practical, material, rather *simple mind.* The main observed characteristic is the lack of imagination.

It is interesting to note that the hand with this short Head Line usually shows the other characteristics which are indicated by this line: short fingers, the general lack of lines and the short square palm.

114 C 3 *The Head Line terminates at the side of the hand in the area of Mars:* Great *intellectual power* in the practical sense, often egoistical.

114 C 4 *The Head Line terminates at the side of the hand in the area of upper Luna:* This is the balanced ending of the Head Line, a combination of *practical and imaginative.* A very successful sign in a hand with willpower (strong Thumb).

114 C 5 *The Head Line terminates at the area of lower Mercury:* This denotes great *success in business* but usually at the expense

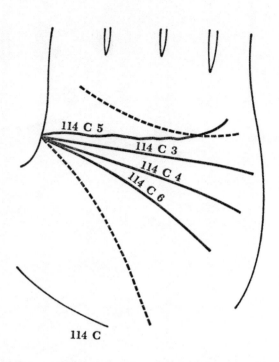

114 C

of others. Seen in the hand of top business executives who have an overpowering wish for money and what it can buy.

114 C 6 *The Head Line terminates at the area of Luna:* This is the termination necessary for successful fiction writers. The *creative* ability is wholly in the *imagination.*

In a poor hand the imagination may run away and create insanity.

The term "poor hand" in this case means a hand showing a lack of logic, so that there is a possibility of reality and the imaginary becoming mixed up. The lack of logic is shown by a short second phalanx of the Thumb. The negative quality is further stressed by a soft hand and super-flexible fingers.

114 D *Branches from the Head Line in the Major Hand:* Branching from the Head Line indicates that the influence of the

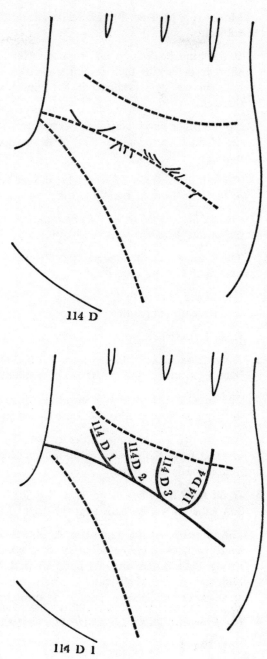

114 D

114 D 1

Mount to which the branch leads affects the thoughts of the subject.

If the branches sweep up from the Head Line but are too short to determine their direction clearly, it means that small constructive ideas originate in the mind but are not followed through.

On the other hand, very small branches sweeping down from the Head Line mean a period of depression of a very minor nature.

These branches will be seen with similar very small branches in the Life Line at the same time period.

114 D 1 *Head Line branches to or from Jupiter:* This adds pride, ambition and *leadership* to the hand.

The form which the leadership will take is seen in the direction of the Head Line itself.

Head Line sweeps *to Mercury-Mars:* in business, finance and mechanical occupations.

Head Line sweeps *to Luna:* in the arts, literature, the occult.

114 D 2 *Head Line branches to or from Saturn:* Do not confuse the Fate Line with a branch to or from the Head Line.

The Mount of Saturn is a negative Mount. It depresses the thinking because it adds the sense of *gloom* and the fatalistic.

Any branch to or from Saturn into or from the Head Line detracts from the quality of the Head Line in that a certain impotence is generated.

114 D 3 *Head Line branches to or from Apollo:* Do not confuse the Sun Line with a branch from the Head Line.

The influence of the Mount of Apollo is felt. It denotes the overpowering *wish for fame.* It is a good marking with a strong Thumb and directed hand since the goal can then be achieved. In the weak hand, it means the wish to be noticed at any cost and is seen among the most infamous criminals.

114 D 4 *Head Line branches to or from Mercury:* Do not confuse

[146]

the Mercury Line (Health Line) with a branch of the Head Line.

This denotes the thinking of the Mount of Mercury imposed upon the hand.

A strong sense for *business and science*. The negative, weak hand here shows the wish for deceit.

114 D 5 *A long straight Head Line branches to Luna:* With willpower and logic indicated by the Thumb, this is the mark of straight "A" students. All subjects come easily to them and they *excel in their studies.*

The ultimate success of these straight "A" students is indicated by the Fate Line, the Sun Line and the Life Line.

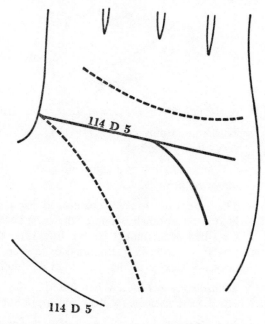

114 D 5

114 D 5

114 D 6 *A sloping Head Line branches to Luna* in a fork formation:

This strengthens the imaginative qualities of Luna, and given a good hand it is the strongest mark found in the hand of the *greatest fiction writers.*

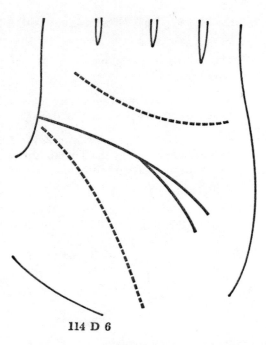

114 D 6

114 D 7 *A branch from the Head Line runs into the Heart Line:*
This branch may cut the Fate Line or Sun Line. It must be
very clearly marked.

It is an indication of danger and is seen when there is a strong
threat of physical harm.

The Life Line must be examined for breaks in the Major
Hand. This branch is one of the corroborating marks to look
for when event marks on the Life Line show danger to the
life. It is also seen in the hand of the reasonable person who
does not recognize the danger in a situation.

114 E *Multiple Head Lines:* When found in the Major Hand, a dual
Head Line indicates a near schizophrenic personality.

In a good hand it is the mark of a *dual personality,* extremely
agile of mind.

In a bad hand it is the sign of the madman, violent with a
straight Head Line, or autistic with a sloping Head Line in
the Major Hand.

[148]

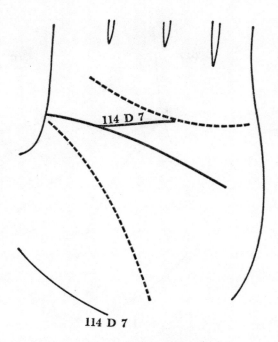

114 D 7

114 D 7

114 F *Spacing of Head and Heart Lines:* When I examine a hand or a print, one of the first things I observe is how the Head Line and the Heart Line divide the entire hand. The line that becomes *displaced* toward the other is the influencing line. In the same way, when the spacing becomes very wide it is again the line that is displaced which gives the determining characteristic.

114 F 1 *The Head Line and Heart Line are close to each other* in middle Mars under Saturn and Apollo: This gives the character the influence of the feelings over the mind. It is a good sign in human terms, a bad sign for a businessman or politician.

114 F 2 *The Head Line and Heart Line are widely separated* in middle Mars under Saturn and Apollo: This is the sign of *cold, calculating thought.* Very strong in an independent hand. It strengthens abstract thought in mathematical minds with logic and a straight Head Line, and also in psychic types with the deep sloping Head Line.

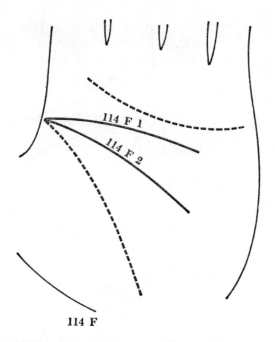

114 F

When I observe that the Head and Heart Lines are widely separated—when I observe the lack of feeling—I follow a routine to pinpoint its meaning to others. For instance, when the Life and Head Lines are also widely separated we are dealing with the extreme of the cold calculator who will take any chance. These people are potentially quite harmful.

My next check is the Thumb for drive and logic. Logic is hardly ever found in a hand with widely separated Head and Heart Lines. The two are mutually exclusive. With a great amount of willpower or the despotic Thumb, the danger is increased for society.

My next check is for intelligence, which shows in the direction, length and ending of the Head Line.

In the same way, whenever I observe any quality in a hand, I follow through in a similar manner to come up with the complete analysis.

114 G   *The quality of the Head Line*

114 G 1 *The smooth unbroken Head Line:* This is the normal appearance of the Head Line, indicating the absence of catastrophic events except as noted on the broken Life Line.

114 G 2 *The chained Head Line:* This is the mark of *vacillation*. Inconsistency of thought.

114 G 3 *The Head Line with islands:* This is an event marking denoting *physical injury* to the head or mental injury (see sections 23 and 25 C).

114 G 4 *The Head Line with breaks:* This is an event marking (see section 24).

114 G 5 *Absence of Head Line:* In the Major Hand, this is an event marking (see section 25).

When seen in the Minor Hand, it means that the missing line is actually the Head Line, or a joined Head and Heart Line. The inherited trait is a *total lack of affection*.

This combined line is often seen in the Minor Hand of abandoned children, if the abandonment was caused by lack of affection.

114 H *The Head Line in Major Handtypes:* The normal Head Line for the Major Handtypes is as follows:

114 H 1 *The straight Head Line* belongs with the practical or square hand: It follows from the above that a sloping Head Line in a square hand is much more meaningful than in other handtypes.

It adds imagination to the execution of work. These people work and think in an imaginative manner. This combination makes good composers, designers and architects if the entire hand is indicative of the creative process.

114 H 2 *The slightly sloping Head Line* belongs with the tapered hand with spatulate fingers: A straight Head Line on this hand means an excess of practicality. The normally active and inventive mind of the spatulate fingers is unduly checked by a straight Head Line.

If a very sloping Head Line is found on the tapered hand, we find that the inventive and psychic powers are heightened.

[151]

114 H 3 *The much sloping Head Line* belongs with the philosophic and psychic hands: The main effect when the Head Line goes straight across the hand is that the mind becomes extremely critical. The criticism is that of the philosopher: finding fault with the thinking of people, not with their work.

In the purely psychic hands it is a great exception to find a Head Line without slope or running straight across the palm. If a psychic hand is found with the straight Head Line, great confusion is the result and the visionary quality alternates with bursts of practical efforts, usually in the arts.

115 *The Heart Line as character marking:* The normal course of the Heart Line through the palm is from a point under Jupiter or Saturn to the edge of the hand under Mercury or to the percussion. It denotes the emotions and feelings of the individual.

The age is read on the Heart Line as illustrated:

115 A *The origin of the Heart Line:* The Heart Line may originate from the center of the Mount of Jupiter, from a point be-

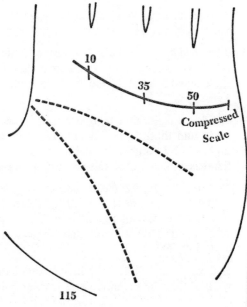

tween Jupiter and Saturn, from Saturn or from any point in the area of Mars.

115 A 1 *The Heart Line originates from the center of the Mount of Jupiter:* This is the best starting point for the Heart Line. It gives the strength of Jupiter to the emotions. Pride, *judgment* and discrimination work in their favor.

These indications make the individual trustworthy, reliable and generally cheerful.

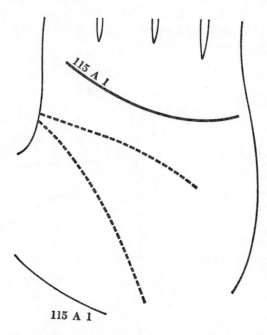

115 A 1

115 A 2 *The Heart Line originates very high on the Mount of Jupiter,* or in the Index Finger: This is the exaggeration of the above and is no longer a good sign. This is a person with too much pride, *too much enthusiasm.* They are blind to faults of others, and though they can be trusted, they will not be able to help themselves or others in case of a real problem. They get hurt easily.

115 A 3 *The Heart Line originates between the Index and Middle Finger:* The emotions with this marking are much more subdued and rational. The sober influence of Saturn is now superimposed on the enthusiasm and emotional leadership of Jupiter. These are *emotionally calm* people.

115 A 4 *The Heart Line originates on Saturn:* A sign of egotistic feelings. The passions are fierce but self-centered and possessive. These qualities in a bad hand indicate utter disregard for the opposite sex.

115 A 5 *The Heart Line originates from the starting point of the Life Line and Head Line:* This is the sign of excessive *calculation* in all affections. This is the sign of the ruthless destroyer and of violent death.

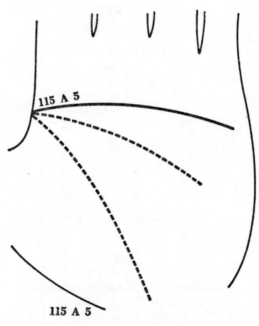

115 A 5

115 A 5

115 B *The course of the Heart Line through the palm:* Once the origin of the Heart Line is established, we check the course for the emotions of the individual.

115 B 1 *The Heart Line curves down close to the Head Line in its course:* This must not be confused with the Head Line curving up toward the Heart Line.

[154]

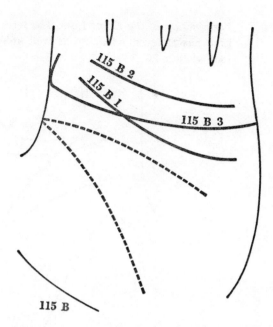

115 B

The difference can be seen by observing any bulge in the central portion of the Head or Heart Lines. The line showing the deformation is the displaced one.

Since the Heart Line is much more indicative of instinctive actions than the Head Line, we deal with the *emotions* (sometimes intuitive actions) *influencing thought.* In this hand the family or loved ones may interfere with cool, logical, business decisions.

115 B 2 *The Heart Line lies high in the palm, far from the Head Line:* Do not confuse this with a very low-lying Head Line.

This is a sign of the individual who will always be *logical* even in affairs involving the emotions.

115 B 3 *The Heart Line crosses the entire hand, from edge to edge:* The sign of extreme and *brutal jealousy* caused by excessive passion. If this Heart Line curves up and runs into the Index Finger, along the edge of the hand, the characteristic is still further worsened and a potentially violent person results.

115 C   *Termination of the Heart Line:* The termination of the Heart Line has an event meaning as well as a character meaning (see section 26 A).

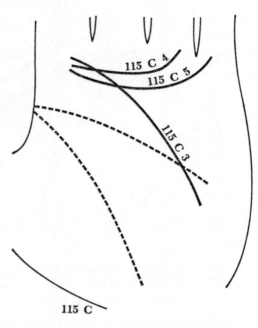

115 C

115 C 1   *Short Heart Line in the Major Hand:* We consider a Heart Line as *short* if it starts at Jupiter or Saturn and stops or fades out under Apollo, before reaching the center of the Ring Finger.

As an event marking it is treated as a break and denotes *heart disease* of a serious nature if in the Major Hand.

115 C 2   *Short Heart Line in the Minor Hand only:* This indicates that one of the parents had a weak heart and was not long-lived.

115 C 3   *The Heart Line terminates on Luna:* If in its course it breaks through the Head Line it indicates *insane jealousy* and subsequent violent action against self or others.

If it does *not* cut through the Head Line, extreme jealousy and imagined hurt is observed.

115 C 4 *The Heart Line terminates on Apollo:* The love for art replaces the love for people when the line *curves up* into Apollo; otherwise, see short Heart Line, section 115 C 1 above.

115 C 5 *The Heart Line terminates up on Mercury:* When the line *curves up* into Mercury, the love for travel and business replaces the love for people.

115 D *Branches to and from the Heart Line in the Major Hand:* When they originate in areas, branches to or from the Heart Line are all in the nature of character modifications. They have no time identification and therefore are not said to branch to or from the Heart Line. They connect the Heart Line with the area which then imparts a meaning to the character.

Only main sources are quoted. Intermediate positions should be interpolated:

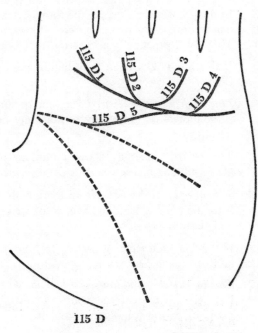

115 D

115 D 1 *A branch to the Heart Line from Jupiter:* This is an excellent mark if it is in the nature of a small fork under the Index Finger. It denotes absolute *honesty,* decency with a warm character.

115 D 2 *A branch to the Heart Line from Saturn:* This is a weakening sign. It *adds uncertainty* and gloom to the emotional outlook. It makes for a harder person to live with.

115 D 3 *A branch to the Heart Line from Apollo:* This sign marks the influence of external stimulation upon the emotions. This branch adds *love for art* to the love for people.

115 D 4 *A branch to the Heart Line from Mercury:* This adds the *love of commerce and travel* to the emotions.

115 D 5 *A branch from the Head Line runs into the Heart Line:* A danger mark (see section 114 D 7).

115 E *The Heart Line is absent in the Major Hand only:* See also section 25 B.

This is a very rare sign and has not been fully documented. In those cases that have come to my attention, they were normal people, very much *emotionally uninvolved with others.* They lived practically aside from society in their own shell.

If this line is absent in both hands, see section 25 A, Simian Line.

115 F *The quality of the Heart Line:* The quality of the Heart Line is the indication of both event markings and character or type markings.

The Heart Line may show a number of different qualities along its length, each with a definite meaning.

115 F 1 *The smooth, unbroken Heart Line:* This, in the Major Hand, is the best Heart Line to have, considering the points of origin and termination.

It then is indicative of *strong feelings for others,* true love and of reasonable nature.

115 F 2 *The broad and shallow Heart Line:* The less-marked Heart Line gives a temperament more involved with itself, less capable of caring for others.

115 F 3 *The chained Heart Line in the Major Hand:* This gives the character an *emotional inconsistency.* People who easily attach and detach themselves from others, during the age indicated.

115 F 4 *Very fine lines joining and leaving the Heart Line:* Unless very clearly marked and standing out, these are not read as branches to the Heart Line. Many very fine lines *crossing* the Heart Line are only indications of an extremely nervous nature.

If the fine lines point up toward the fingers, they denote unusual interest in the opposite sex.

If the fine lines point down toward the wrist, they denote minor disappointments in the sex life.

If the fine lines cross the Heart Line (not to be confused with any of the major lines crossing, as the Fate, Sun or Health Lines) these lines indicate actual interference in the affections or feelings.

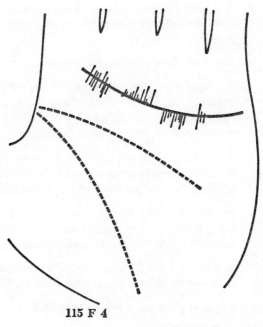

115 F 4

115 F 5 *The Heart Line is very fine and thin toward the edge of the hand:* This is the sign of *sterility.*

115 F 6 *The Heart Line with islands:* This denotes a physical defect in the heart (see section 26 B).

115 G *The Heart Line with breaks:* This is a Heart Line that continues after showing a break.

This is basically an event line: The break denotes a separation between the subject and a loved one, but the personality of the subject should be read through other character marks to see if the separation can be averted or repaired through a change in outlook or attitude.

115 G 1 *A break under Saturn:* Separation through a fatal accident (subject may be foolhardy or reckless).

115 G 2 *A break under Apollo:* Separation through a change of affection to the arts (subject may place love of art over love of people).

115 G 3 *A break under Mercury:* Separation through the wish for fame and money (love for money and fame over love for people).

116 *The Fate Line as character marking*

116 A *A strong Fate Line ascending to the Mount of Jupiter* is an indication of great ambition and *leadership power.* It combines the success indicated by this strong Fate Line and the qualities of the Mount of Jupiter.

116 A 1 If the Fate Line originates from more than one area in the hand, the qualities associated with those areas will be part of the character makeup of the individual.

For instance, two branches making up the origin of the Fate Line, one from Luna and one from Venus, create a personality influenced by the imagination as much as by sex.

116 B *A missing Fate Line or Sun Line* denotes a life without excitement, without joy, without trouble.

117 *The Sun Line as character marking*

The strong Sun Line denotes a *brilliant mind when it is found in the square hand*. It is a good line in the philosophic or psychic hands, where it is usually found as a matter of routine.

The entire hand will indicate whether the strength is in the arts or in worldly affairs. In the practical hand with a straight Head Line and a strong Thumb, it lies in the performing arts or business practice.

In the practical hand with a sloping Head Line to Luna, it lies in the creative arts such as writing, composing and original painting.

118   *Minor character lines:* There is a group of lines that adds special characteristics to the hand:

118 A   *The Line of Intuition in the Major Hand:* This is the line seen in the hands of intuitive people and is more commonly seen in the philosophic and psychic hands.

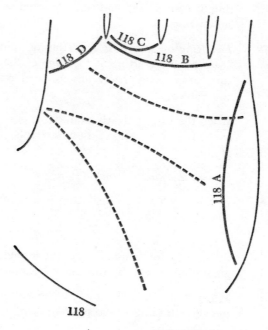

118

This adds intuitive feeling and sometimes prophetic dreaming. These people are very impressionable. It is a very valuable asset to the writer and those dealing with people.

118 B   *The Girdle of Venus in the Major Hand*

118 B 1   *In a square hand* this line takes away some of the strength of the hand and adds a strange quality of sensitivity unusual in the strong hand.

118 B 2   *In the philosophic or psychic hand:* A strengthening factor of the very sensitivity of the subject. This added line makes these people *deeply emotional,* verging toward the hysterical in a weak hand.

118 B 3   *The Girdle of Venus touching the Affection Line:* A bad sign for the relationship. *Abnormal desires* or excessive demands on the love partner cause great conflict.

118 C   *The Ring of Saturn:* This is a total blocking of Saturn, denoting a complete frustration in anything attempted. The ring, if open in the middle, is less unfavorable than the fully closed ring.

118 D   *The Ring of Solomon:* The Ring of Solomon is a very rare, distinct mark starting at the edge of the hand under Jupiter and curving completely around to a point between Jupiter and Saturn.

When the ring is clearly marked, it denotes practical powers in the occult sciences. Serious students of ESP belong in this group.

119   *Special marking on the Mounts*

119 A   *The star,* when seen distinctly, is a reinforcing marking anywhere in the hand.

It must not be composed of the chance crossing of any other lines: The star is one of the minor signs in the hand and is greatly influenced by the general character of the hand.

When a star is seen, analyze the entire hand first and add the star meaning to the positive attributes of the hand.

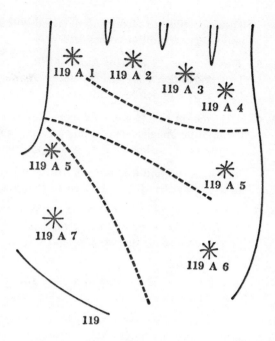

Figure labels: 119 A 1, 119 A 2, 119 A 3, 119 A 4, 119 A 5, 119 A 5, 119 A 7, 119 A 6, 119

119 A 1   *The star on the Mount of Jupiter:* A reinforcing sign at all times, but in Jupiter with a good hand, practical (square), mental (long first phalanx of Index Finger) and when the Mount is centrally located, this produces the highest form of leadership.

119 A 2   *The star on the Mount of Saturn:* A negative sign. The fatalism becomes very pronounced since the star is a strengthening mark. This is a leader again, but fate opposes the very carrier of this hand. The genius is ultimately destroyed.

119 A 3   *The star on the Mount of Apollo:* When seen at the end of the Sun Line, it ends the life on a note of great brilliance.

The struggle for this recognition usually lasts too long for the artist, bringing a bitter sort of happiness.

119 A 4   *The star on the Mount of Mercury:* Brilliance and success in science, late in life. This mark is found on great scientists who ultimately gain recognition.

[163]

These people are always appreciated within their circle, but universal recognition comes late.

119 A 5 *The star on the area of Mars:* Military honors late in life. This is positive (aggressive) under Jupiterian Mars; passive (defensive) under Mercurian Mars.

119 A 6 *The star on the Mount of Luna:* This is a sign of excessive or supreme imagination. In this area the star denotes the borderline between imaginative genius and insanity.

In a literary hand it is the sign of the greatest fiction writers. In a musical hand it is the sign of the greatest composers.

119 A 7 *The star on the Mount of Venus:* This is the star of conquering love. The greatest lovers, the sex conqueror, the unopposed Don Juan, the women who seduce all men, bear this mark.

This power is devastating in a bad hand; the toll is in human souls and lives.

119 B *The triangle as a character marking:* There are various positions where a triangle has a character marking beyond the event marking discussed in section 53.

The triangle is always a positive mark. It must be clearly marked and not made up by three chance lines crossing:

119 B 1 *The triangle on the Mount of Jupiter:* The character mark of the great organizer. The highly successful leader.

119 B 2 *The triangle on the Mount of Saturn:* The expert in occult studies—see also section 53 A.

119 B 3 *The triangle on the Mount of Apollo:* This denotes the *master in the arts,* the self-assured creator, expert musician.

119 B 4 *The triangle on the Mount of Mercury:* The *expert in business,* the top athlete, the financier.

119 B 5 *The triangle on the Area of Mars:* This gives great courage and knowledge in warfare and exploration.

119 B 6 *The triangle on Luna:* The highest level of imagination, the most successful mark for a *writer of fiction.*

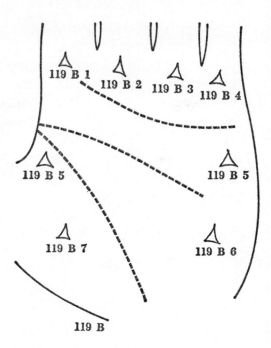

119 B

119 B 7   *The triangle on Venus:* Great *power in love* and sex.

119 C   *Vertical lines on the Mounts:* There is a general rule about vertical and horizontal secondary lines in the hand: *All vertical secondary lines reinforce the hand, all horizontal secondary lines weaken it.* Lines running along the Life Line, Fate Line and Sun Line reinforce those lines; all secondary lines crossing these three lines are detrimental.

The Head and Heart Line are not affected by the major lines (Life, Fate, Sun and Health Lines) cutting them. The only exception is the crossing point of the Life and Health Lines, which indicates the natural life-span.

The same rule holds true for vertical and horizontal lines on the Mounts. Vertical lines reinforce the Mounts; horizontal lines or rings weaken them.

Each Mount has its own meaning (see section 110) which is reinforced by vertical lines on that Mount.

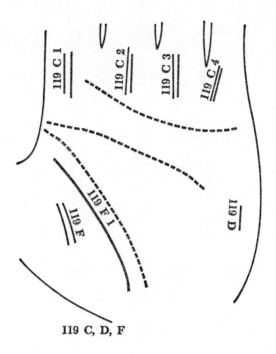

119 C, D, F

There are many hands that are crisscrossed with fine lines, which denote only a nervous condition.

These lines are never read as event or character lines. The character-indicating lines *stand out* quite clearly apart from these hairlines.

Again, we read only the Major Hand as indicative of the subject. The Minor Hand shows the inherited potential:

119 C 1 *Vertical lines on the Mount of Jupiter:* Vertical markings on Jupiter, if the hand is not generally filled with fine lines, is an indication of success as a leader.

The Jupiterian is a *leader* in politics, religion and the military.

If the vertical lines are seen in the Major Hand, they denote a positive attitude in life, especially active in religion and politics. These people easily preconceive ideas from which they will not budge. Excellent with a strong and logical hand, one with a well-marked Head Line.

If the vertical lines are seen in the Minor Hand only, this is an inherited trait which is not used.

119 C 2 *Vertical lines on the Mount of Saturn:* If the hand is not generally filled with fine lines, this is a multiple Fate Line and denotes success in later life.

The finer lines flanking a well-marked vertical Fate Line on Saturn only indicate that the success is derived later in life from serious studies and applied personal talent.

If the Fate Line has started lower in the hand, see section 29 up.

119 C 3 *Vertical lines on the Mount of Apollo:* If the hand is not generally filled with fine lines, this is a multiple Sun Line and denotes success in the creative arts in later life.

Fine lines flanking a well-marked Sun Line on the Mount of Apollo add the strength of creative thought and retention developing later in life.

119 C 4 *Vertical lines on the Mount of Mercury:* If the hand is not completely filled with fine lines these are the marks of success in business.

The vertical lines we are considering here are the short lines on the inside of the start of the Health Line. They reinforce the qualities for study and business and channel the restless energy of the Mercurian type. We see this mark in the lawyer and medical student.

Note that lines coming from the Affection Line are located closer to the percussion of the hand. These lines are so-called *Children's Lines* and are said to indicate the number of children one has.

119 D *Vertical lines on the Mount of Luna:* These lines are easily confused with the Line of Intuition and the Health Line. If a few clearly marked vertical lines are seen in the area of Luna, we are dealing with Travel Lines. See Part One, section 61.

119 E *Vertical lines on the areas of Mars:* The areas of Mars are the areas of mechanical objects. There are no vertical lines in the areas of Mars which do not form part of the Fate, Sun, Health or Intuition Lines.

The vertical lines that end in the areas of Mars are always considered connected with *events* seen in the Life, Fate and Sun Lines (see section 12 C for example).

The Martian character is extremely strong and emphasis is unnecessary and never seen.

See also Croix Mystique, section 123.

119 F *Vertical lines on the Mount of Venus:* All lines on the Mount of Venus are Influence Lines denoting relationships with other people.

The lines following the Life Line on the thumbside, which are not considered *Companion Lines* to the Life Line (section 18 B), are considered the *Lines of Mars,* since when extended they originate in the area of Mars-Jupiter.

119 F 1 *The Mars Line:* This line is *much deeper* and more distinct than Influence Lines that run along the Life Line. It is the line of the fighter, and gives great physical strength and health.

It is also often found in the hand with a weak, sometimes broken Life Line. It carries this hand safely past the danger to life and is treated as an event marking (section 17 B 1). A *crossing line involving the Mars Line* is treated as if the Mars Line were the Life Line.

120 *Negative markings on the Mounts*

120 A *Horizontal lines on the Mounts*—Major Hand only: Again, the general rule is true that all horizontal or horizontally crossing lines have a negative meaning.

The only exception is when the horizontal lines are part of a square, which is a repair mark. These lines will be no longer than the vertical lines making up the two other sides of the square.

120 A 1 *Horizontal lines on the Mount of Jupiter:* This is a blocked Jupiter condition, negating the leadership qualities. It is a character trait that makes it unwanted or impossible to be the leader.

It is also seen in the hands of people who do not want to follow a leadership or religious dictum.

120 A 2 *Horizontal lines on the Mount of Saturn:* This is a variation of the Ring of Saturn (section 118 C). Again, total blocking of Saturn. It is a very bad sign in the Major Hand, since it defeats all efforts the person makes.

120 A 3 *Horizontal lines on the Mount of Apollo:* Blocking of this Mount indicates negative forces in the creative talent. Do not confuse these lines with the Girdle of Venus (section 118 B) which is *curved*. Blocking lines are horizontal and short.

Eye defects are connected with blocking horizontal lines on Apollo, or any abnormality in the Sun Line near the Mount.

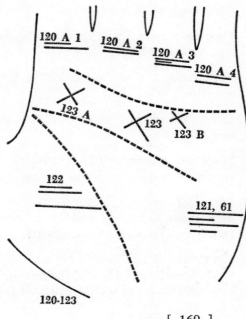

120 A 4   *Horizontal lines on the Mount of Mercury:* Not to be confused with the Affection Line (section 43). These small lines must be seen on the inside of the Mount. They must not come from the percussion, for in that case they are Affection Lines.

When the blocking horizontal lines appear on Mercury, it means that the studies are stopped by external force.

It is a bad sign for athletes, businessmen and all students since it stops the energy normally associated with Mercury necessary for success.

121   *Horizontal lines on the Mount of Luna:* These are also Travel Lines. The same event markings apply as for vertical lines on this Mount. These lines start at the percussion and go into the Mount of Luna (see section 61).

122   *Horizontal lines on the Mount of Venus:* These lines should not cross the Life Line, or they are considered event markings.

122 A   Forming a *square,* they are a preserving mark against trouble through a sex involvement.

122 B   Forming a *grille,* they denote trouble in sex relations (see also section 124 F).

122 C   Not crossing nor touching any other lines, they weaken the sex drive.

122 D   If these lines cross the Life Line, they are event marks (section 12).

123   *The Croix Mystique:* This is a separately marked cross in the center of the middle area of Mars.

123 A   *The Croix Mystique toward the Jupiter area of Mars: Curiosity about occult phenomena.* A person who looks for knowledge in a nonscientific manner.

123 B   *The Croix Mystique high in the area of Mars, near the Heart Line: Superstitious curiosity.* Observe the quality of the Head Line and Thumb to see the extent of superstition.

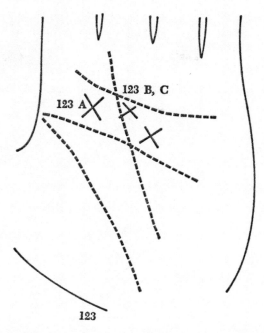

123

123 C   *The Croix Mystique touching the Fate Line:* Study of the occult is the main interest in life. See also Ring of Solomon (section 118 D).

124   *The grille modifying the Mounts:* The grille is a weakening or negative mark. It is formed by three or more lines crossing at about right angles.

124 A   *The grille on the Mount of Jupiter:* This is a character mark, denoting snobbism or excessive pride. If an event line from Venus ends in a grille on this Mount, I have found it to mean confinement of a voluntary form such as the convent.

124 B   *The grille on the Mount of Saturn:* This gives a strong sense of the gruesome, a morbid outlook. An event line from Venus ending in this grille is a sure sign of some severe accident in the family.

124 C   *The grille on the Mount of Apollo:* This means *conceit*. It is a hindrance to all forms of success, not only in the arts.

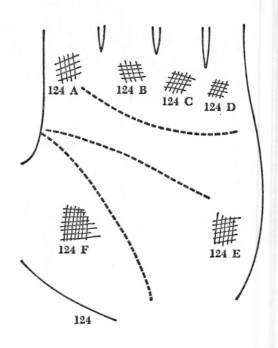

An event line from Venus ending in a grille on Apollo indicates an eye injury.

124 D   *The grille on the Mount of Mercury:* This is a block in the active, extroverted character of this Mount. The negative activity shows in a volatile pseudo businesslike manner.

This is the character that cheats itself and others, usually involuntarily.

124 E   *The grille on the Mount of Luna:* Luna is the seat of imagination and travel. The blocking of these qualities by a grille formation results in a person who is constantly discontent and wishes to be elsewhere with better people.

124 F   *The grille on the Mount of Venus:* A blocking of the sense of honor in love, lack of self-control, makes this the nymphomaniac, the pimp and the flirt.

[172]

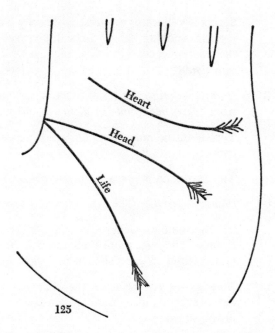

125

Note that there are usually a great many crossing lines found on the Mount of Venus: These are not to be read as constituting a grille.

125　*The tassel ending of a line:* The tasseled ending on the Life Line, Head Line, Heart Line or Fate Line is a weakening form of the line.

It is a commonly seen ending for the Life Line, where it denotes gradual loss of energy in old age.

126　*Illnesses according to type:* The *pure type* characteristics that go with the various hands—Jupiterian, Saturnian, Apollonian, Mercurian, Martian, Lunarian and Venusian—include certain diseases that they are prone to.

Pure types are described in section 110 under "Mounts."

126 A　*Illnesses—Jupiter:* The Jupiterian enjoys life and its contributions. They enjoy food, and the most common typically Jupiterian ailments have to do with their digestion.

Secondary illnesses are usually directly traceable to their eating and smoking habits. Since Jupiterians smoke excessively, the consequences are often seen as extreme cases of *lung infection.*

126 B   *Illnesses—Saturn:* The Saturnian is *nervous* and suffers much from *bone, back and leg ailments* and ulcers.

Typical of the pure Saturnian are varicose veins and rheumatism.

The Saturnian is not a healthy type but is long-lived at that.

126 C   *Illnesses—Apollo:* The Apollonian is a healthy person.

The outstanding weakness of Apollo is a disposition to eye trouble. They get more than their share of rheumatic fever, or infections in general to which they are sensitive.

126 D   *Illnesses—Mercury:* Like the Saturnian, the Mercurian is nervous in a much more outwardly way. The difference is in the showing.

Big business and ulcers are a joint venture of the pure Mercurian.

Secondary illnesses are mostly derived from the intensely nervous drive that upsets their digestive tract no end.

126 E   *Illnesses—Mars:* This is the eating and drinking type, generally healthy and quite robust.

Intestinal problems, respiratory diseases and circulatory ailments are their weaknesses.

126 F   *Illnesses—Luna:* Another unhealthy pure type. Typical troubles are kidney and gallstones, and problems with the lower intestines.

Much sensitivity to infections, acutely nervous.

126 G   *Illnesses—Venus:* Pure Venusians are a very robust type. No typical ailment is ascribed to them. They suffer as others from infectious diseases.

COMBINATIONS

127　　The combination of characteristics creates most of the problems in the analysis of a hand. When we read events we have none of these problems because they are chronologically located on the main lines. Events have only one meaning and are thus more simple to explain. But when we deal with personality we are faced with combinations.

I have previously suggested that we look at the charts for the number and write down the underlined characteristic descriptive for that particular marking. When we analyze the descriptions we then find some characteristics cancelling themselves as a matter of routine. These self-cancelling character traits are usually minor, however; the outstanding characteristics of a person are never self-cancelling, but they do come in combinations.

For example, look at the Thumb: willpower and logic. The willpower cannot be cancelled, neither can logic.

Look at the Fate Line: Success cannot be cancelled. However, it is entirely possible to have no Fate Line and a large amount of willpower. Why no success? The answer is usually found in the Health Line.

These combinations are usually most puzzling for the beginning—and often for the more experienced—hand-line reader. The following combination problems deal with only the most common characteristics.

127 A　　*Fate and Sun Line combinations:* Traditional palmists have attached so much importance to the Fate and Sun Lines that it is worthwhile to consider their value in interpreting success in addition to their event meaning—which has been fully explored in the first part of this book.

First of all, the subject has to have a clear-cut idea of personal success. This is part of an intelligence factor contained in the Head Line (section 114 up).

Without a clear idea of success, there will be no well-formed Fate or Sun Line. This accounts for the easily detected Fate or Sun Line among performers (although not necessarily well marked).

The hand of the successful person who does not have either a Fate or Sun Line accentuates the fact that there was no anticipation or wish for success in any preceding period.

Combination factors show us the *reason* for the success or lack of success. Combinations are found in the Thumb and Fingers and the supporting Mounts, hand shapes and lines.

Fate or Sun Line is long and well marked: This is the positive sign of accomplishment. To analyze where the success originates, we have to find supporting combination characteristics.

127 B   *Thumb combination characteristics:* Success comes from willpower and logic. We do not need to channel or encourage the large Thumb.

If there is *no sign of willpower* and still a well-marked Fate or Sun Line, then we shall find the reason for success in a well-shaped Life Line without illnesses and very often in a very low sloping Head Line that indicates great imagination. Or success may be seen to be due to the influence of friends and family, which is shown in the origin of the Fate Line (section 29).

Remember that instant and unexpected success does not create a well-marked long Fate or Sun Line; it will only be marked at that period of life where it occurs. The long well-marked Sun or Fate Line shows the realization of hoped-for recognition.

127 C   *Absence of the Sun or Fate Line:* The absent lines do not necessarily constitute a lack of success, as noted above. Any success would be much more instantaneous—it was not worked for, it was not expected. When the lines are totally absent, the emotional personality is often lacking.

In analyzing character I consider only the lines that are present, not the absence of certain lines, with the exception of the Fate and Sun Lines. When I now find a very strong Head

[176]

Line sloping into Luna (section 114 B 3) and a strong Thumb (section 101 up) but a total lack of Sun and Fate Lines, I have to start considering failure and its cause. This is a bad combination showing probable emotional or physical weakness underlying the problem. Most palm readers shy away from any negative markings in the hand, but my research is mainly concerned with the organization of lines for interpretation and I consider this merely as one of the possible groupings. When we find the cause for the lines, we shall also find the way to avoid these groupings.

The absence of the Fate or Sun Line and a well-developed Thumb and Fingers, especially in the philosophical and psychic hand shapes, is a very rare combination and bears close scrutiny. I carefully inspect the quality of the Health Line and Life Line for visible aberrations. Remember that either the Fate or Sun Line seem to fulfill similar functions and are acceptable indicators of achievement. If we want to see the areas of success, we have to consider the supporting Fingers and Mount markings.

127 D   *Head Line combinations:* We have seen in section 114 H that the Head Line has certain characteristics, according to the type of hand in which it is found. The Head Line is not only the indicator of the mentality of the subject but also a combining factor in evaluating the eventual success of the subject.

All main groups can be found with the three basic types of Head Line, and with or without pronounced Fate or Sun Line. (I am now neglecting the Fate and Sun Line markings, since they show the extent of success as I mentioned above and will see how each form of Head Line will direct each main group.) I will indicate the main types of Head Line with letters A, B and C, which will indicate the Straight, Slightly Sloping and Much Sloping Head Lines respectively. I shall also indicate the main groups by their initials: J–Jupiter, S–Saturn, A–Apollo, M–Mercury, Ma–Mars, L–Luna and V–Venus.

Neglecting intensity of success, we then find the following results:

J–A   A strong leader, very practical, often political

J–B   A leader, more idealistic, often religious

J–C   A leader, idealistic, quasi-religious, more tolerant

S–A   A sober mathematical mind, usually quite analytical

S–B   A skeptical, practical but more tolerant person, but still with a rather morose view of the world

S–C   Much more fantasy can be ascribed to this combination, and we can find a person who can poke fun at gloom or write horror stories

A–A   Creative artists, and the originators of fashion with the emphasis on the practical

A–B   Creative art, with the emphasis on the esthetical

A–C   Creative art for the sake of form or effect

M–A   The leader in business, merchant, social scientist

M–B   The inventor of practical products, the merchant, the quick wit

M–C   This formation produces the business theoretician, the counselor in government on trade and economy; superimposes imagination on business thinking

Ma–A   Strategic and practical thinking makes this a strong commercial hand, quite aggressive

Ma–B   A commercial and strategic hand with an overtone of originality; unusual tactics that can be highly successful

Ma–C   Quite unconventional and rarely seen combination. Both in commerce and the army exceptionally agile in evasive tactics and pulling fast punches

L–A   Mathematical ability, abstract thought (rare)

L–B Writing ability, abstract thinking and fantasy dominate

L–C Fully developed fantasy, highly imaginative

V–A A realistic look at love and life, warmth tempered by intellect

V–B A warm person, love for people and with an outgoing personality

V–C The seeker of ideals, hard to satisfy (rare)

In summing up: Neglecting the Thumb series of combinations and also neglecting the Fate and Sun Line series of combinations, we see that the Head Line series gives us the direction of the main group, varying from the practical (Head Line type A) to the mental (Head Line type C).

Other various combination series to consider are:

The Health Line, nail and Life Line condition series

The finger length series

The finger position series

The markings on the Mount series

The hand shape series

I will emphasize again that all the character traits of the subject will show themselves when the numbered lines on the charts are identified and the meanings that are italicized are written down.

Part 3

Analysis

I live by my hand print. It tells me much about myself that I want to know, and the same knowledge will be gained by anyone. I may not always like what I see, but I must accept the basic outlines of life and improve wherever I can.

Is it valuable to know future trends? If the trend can be corrected, I would say that it is; if it cannot, I should not worry about it. Then it becomes my lot.

Most palmists are asked "What can you tell me about my career?" or "Will I be successful (happy, rich, healthy)?" or "How can I tell if so-and-so is unfaithful (miserly, cruel, a loser)?" or some variant of the above. These subjects are not asking about event lines or character marks; they are interested in topics—and ask the palmist to know immediately which features to check. Therefore, this section is alphabetized into various topics that commonly arise.

First, however, a few words about analysis:

* The hand shows us *potential* limitations, not the *actual* ones, since I have seen many lines and character marks appear and disappear from hands.

* Major lines have no need to change since repair lines and —in the case of character marks—variations can be introduced that modify the original meaning.

* Remember that when a subject asks "Will I be happy?" the palmist should not answer with even a qualified "yes" or "no" *but rather explain how the subject may best achieve satisfaction and fulfillment,* given the present hand print.

Which of these areas can we strengthen in a positive manner? It is conceivable that psychiatry with chemical or other treatments may improve the hand lines in a dramatic way. Or a less severe case could be channelled positively by finding all the markings in the hand that are *similarly* directed. Too many failures have been caused by encouraging ability in too many different directions.

* We have a starting point if we can create interest in something *even if it is only to show change in the hand lines*

[183]

as can be demonstrated by consecutive hand prints. I know of no better way to help people than to tell them that they are bound to improve, *if the capacity is shown inherited in the Minor Hand.* But if the signs are solidly unfavorable, we wonder what to say—if anything. Much future study has to be done to explain these problems that show up so dramatically in the lines of the Major Hand.

Abnormal Mentality: If we encounter an abnormal set of lines in the hand, a grouping that is clearly different from any which we have encountered in our experience, we deal with an abnormality.

This abnormality in the hand invariably corresponds with a deviation in the mental or physical condition of the person. When the Head Line runs along an abnormal course and dips deep into Luna, when there are grilles or stars on the Mount of Luna, and when the logic is small, we may deal with a mental aberration.

As long as the deviation does not affect society, only the individual is concerned. Sometimes a great tragedy is taking place, known to only a very few people, since the abnormally lined hand does not communicate on a dependable level.

The abnormal mind may *seem* to be saying what we hear, but in actuality they are communicating around us. They very often also communicate with themselves in the same way, which is why I feel that the availability of proper internal connections is a must for happiness.

The so-called *negative character marks* show themselves by excessive downward sloping of the Head Line or by markings on the area of Luna, by deformation of the Head Line itself, the Thumb lacking logic, the extreme nervous condition of the entire hand or an imbalance, a contradiction in the hand that corresponds to a contradiction in the mind.

The contradictory hand corresponds to a split personality on all levels: It is important to note if the contradictions create anxiety or unhappiness.

If there is enough energy or willpower and enough logic available, there may be a way to guide this hand. It must be admitted that the guiding is through an *internal connection only stimulated by the recognition of the dichotomy.*

We assume that the contradiction can be divided in two parts: a positive and a negative. Remember that willpower stimulates *both* the good and bad parts of the hand. It becomes a matter of determining which are the good parts and which the bad; positive markings are easier to strengthen, in most cases, than negative. In my experience, good or positive character markings have a habit of improving naturally, while negative markings have to be *willfully* strengthened. *It takes negative strength* to weaken the hand; it *needs nothing* to improve a hand naturally.

I will say to the unhappy unbalanced person: "Try to *strengthen* the positive markings. *Forget* the negative markings. These negative marks *will not* strengthen naturally, but you *can* improve the positive marks. This poses a task of course, requiring energy, and I can only hope that you have enough channelled energy available to show an improvement in your hand print over a period of no more than a year."

Positive markings are Success Lines (sections 10, 30, 33, 38, 53, 119) and a *directed hand.* Unfortunately the entire problem posed here originates in an unchannelled, or worse, a contradictory hand.

The contradictory hand has a hand shape that does not correspond to the Head Line normally seen in such hands (section 114 H), also finger shapes not corresponding with the Head Line configuration.

In the contradictory hand there are at all times opposing characteristics indicated by two or more markings—the reason for the potential problem. With abundant willpower, however, the two or more character traits will occur at different moments and not fight each other simultaneously.

For instance: a person may imagine himself or herself to be a failure. It requires intelligence to consider oneself anything to begin with. This would be evident in long pointed fingers, with the first phalanges more than normally developed (sections 102, 105, 107).

Logic would be lacking, except in the case of the double or chained Head Line. Also the imagination area of Luna would show unusual development. We are dealing with a double mind: the real one (apparent to the outsider) and the imaginary one, shown by this strange development of the area of Luna, in the Head Line slope (sometimes indicating suicide) and in Venus-to-Luna event lines (section 12 E 4).

Achievement is shown by a rather limited number of markings and lines: The potential for achievement requires energy, a certain minimal amount of logic and a *directed* hand. This means that the energy of the hand is not dissipated by a multitude of efforts that are undertaken simultaneously. It is the opposite of the mixed hand. The *directed hand* is a very successful sign by itself, all other indications being equal. The direction is *not* the direction the person necessarily will take; it is merely the potential direction. If no lines change in the Major Hand, then it will also become the actual direction.

Again, the Minor Hand shows us the inherited traits, which can be seen as changed or changing in the Major Hand. The chance of successful results is seen by the presence of Success Lines on the Mounts in the Minor Hand (section 119 C).

The Major Hand again will give the change away from predisposition. It is therefore extremely important for the checking both of the trends of capability and achievement to make comparative hand prints at regular intervals. Any deviation in the wrong direction will become evident after a very short period.

There is no other manner I can think of that can guide us so decidedly. If a teacher says, "You are doing well," it is the word of another person. But when the hand print tells you so, there can be no doubt in your mind. Of course, the meaning of the term "well" depends on the wishes of the subject, but the hand print will not let itself be influenced by a mere wish.

Compatibility: The answer to the question "What kind of person should I look for as my partner in life?" is partially contained in the hand lines and hand shape. The questions of instinctive attraction and physical attractiveness, however, lie outside the realm of the topographical hand-line reader. But apart from these two topics there are a number of important clues that will benefit both partners in an attachment.

Compatibility between people hinges on a number of phenomena in the hand lines. To begin with, both partners' overall hands should show similar health, evident in the appearance of the Life Line and Health Line. The easy manner in which to compare two hands for health is to write down the numbers applying to each Major Hand. For instance, if one of the hands shows markings on the Life Line corresponding to section 15 or 113 A, then the compatible hand should have numbers 15 and 113 A as the corresponding number. This would give *similar compatibility.* Some *opposite compatibility* exists, also easily discernible by comparing section codes.

The second compatibility to look for is one of *events.* This is a very strange form of compatibility *found in no other way* than by comparing two hands.

Many people deeply involved with each other have sometimes been driven apart by *events* surrounding them—war, death, inherited wealth and lawsuits are just a few examples of these problems. We cannot always predict events, but we can project at which time in life the people will be sensitive to outside pressure.

If one hand shows sensitivity to outside events (not the extremely nervous hand with fine worry lines, which is explained in section 12), and the partners' hand does not, then these hands are not compatible. Outside influences will soon break up the relationship.

The third compatibility to look for is the similarity in main characteristics. We find the best matches in the cases of *close character form,* or *opposite but complementary.*

The *close character* is easily verified by comparing descriptive section numbers from 101 up, which should basically correspond.

Note, however, that it is doubtful if some markings should correspond in the hands of two partners. For instance, stubbornness should not be shown in both partners' hands, nor aggression (section 101 B 1 A) nor a flirtatious character (section 47)—which should not occur even in one hand.

The hand of the liar (negative elementary hand, section 109 A) is a bad hand in either partner. Therefore, the negative markings should ideally be absent in both partners.

The *complementary character* form is much harder to analyze because it is not an easy task to determine which are complementary characteristics throughout the period of attachment.

The sections that should show this complementary character are those dealing with the *Thumb and Fingers, but not the knots in the Fingers* (a messy husband does not complement an orderly wife), the *hand shape* and the character of the lines.

Very important are the Travel Lines in both hands, which should not differ since both hands should show equal *desire* for travel, not to mention being in the same place at the same time.

Varied interest markings: A very good team can exist when one is mathematically minded and the other inclined to languages. Providing they are receptive to *goodwill,* these people will bring something from the outside into their union. Compatibility is of long term when it is constantly fed with new impressions; boredom destroys. Ignorance engenders boredom. An ignorant mind cannot expect to survive alongside a developed one. Ignorance and wisdom are opposites, but not compatible in the long run.

Energy: One of the foremost characteristics upon which many of the others depend is our *energy,* or *willpower.* This is revealed in the first phalanx of the Thumb. We are born with a certain amount of energy. I see many people who live a tranquil life, with a short, unenergetic first phalanx of the Thumb. They do not *want* more than what they can attain easily, and are very happy with their surroundings.

The large Thumb, with its excess of willpower, meets its adversary who also has a large Thumb, the strong wills clash resoundingly.

It is also possible to evaluate, from the Life Line, periods of a subject's life where the energy level ebbs and surges forward. This is a purely inherited trend. Some hands start off very strong on action and gradually diminish in later life, with periods of ups and downs. Other hands start on a low note and build up momentum throughout life and go out in a blaze of glory. And, of course, there exist all the variations between these two extremes.

If the Life Line shows more activity in the Minor Hand in later life than at the beginning, there is every reason to suspect a gradual *rise of activity*. If the person has reached about 30 years of age, then the Major Hand will show signs of agreement or disagreement. If the Minor Hand is more active than the Major Hand, there is a fault at work in the subject.

If, on the other hand, the Minor Hand shows more activity early in the Life Line markings, then we are dealing with a potential decrease of activity in later age.

Again, the Major Hand must agree or disagree with inherited traits to give the personal equation up or down.

The Future: Topographical palmistry cannot predict the absolute future, but it can predict what can occur if no corrective steps are taken. This means that there are certain positive steps a person can take to avoid encountering a fate predicted by the inherited makeup.

Unfortunately, there are no known methods at this present time that can alleviate all negative traits, but there are many negative destructive traits that *can* and *should* be corrected by anyone who is aware of them. See *Negative Markings* section 120.

Happiness: When analyzing the hand for happiness, not success, look for the *energy level* and the *logic level* upon which the person operates.

When I see a well-directed hand with little drive but logic in abundance, I will state that the hand is potentially a happy one, since it will accept its own shortcomings. Unhappy people are, among others, those who *see* and lament their own failings.

If lack of logic and a large amount of energy can be a source of unhappiness, lack of energy is sometimes equally frustrating. This purely genetic quality is judged from the Thumb. A person who is physically ill may temporarily suffer from lack of energy, but will return to the former energy level after the illness subsides.

We must not confuse the *nervous* hand with the energetic hand. The nervous hand has many lines crossing all over and it defeats energy (from the Thumb) by *un*directing it. The nervous hand does become happy and unhappy, but with extremely quick fluctuations. The person unhappy today will be happy tomorrow, and unhappy again the day after.

For these people there is no answer except: "Your happiness will fluctuate greatly throughout your life." We rarely find great *logic* in the very nervous hand, since that would calm down the subject by its very presence. The only hand that has a chance to grow to happiness, and not be ignorant, is the disciplined, directed, *logical hand.*

Since it therefore appears that this energy level is inherited, it should not be cause for unhappiness. It is fairly obvious that with great logic this shortcoming can be understood—and with a lack of logic the attention would never be drawn to this defect. Happy people are thoroughly satisfied with themselves. The greatest unhappiness occurs in the border area, where medium energy and medium logic are found.

Also look carefully for the *direction* of the hand, and last but not least, the threat of negative future markings. These negative future markings may repair themselves, but even if the markings are event markings outside the personal domain, the threat usually requires *positive corrective action* on the part of the subject.

Here we find one of the greatest clues to happiness: the potential to correct a threatened negative condition that is clearly shown as a future flaw in the character.

We are all more or less subject to periods of emotional ups and downs. These periods over a longer time span are shown in the hand. If we know that we shall go through a strong period of our life, we can take advantage of it; conversely, if we know that we have to wait to arrive at such a period, we can accept our present condition. Of course, I have analyzed hands that were quite without any periodic success markings, but these were people not worried about life and if not ecstatically happy, were generally very content.

The *unhappy* hand has the potential to become a happy hand, much more so than the mixed, indifferent hand.

Fortunately, people will not often ask the question "Will I become happy?" It takes great effort to change the direction of the hand when another path has been already taken. It is of little use to say to an accountant, "You would have been happy if you had become an architect." It is far better to say, "I believe that your happiness will be enhanced by travel or reading about great works of architecture"—in other words, to suggest that this person create a vicarious world in which he can spend some happy years.

The person who asks, "How may I *now* become happy?" can be guided, providing such a person is physically healthy.

From the preceding, it might appear that the ultimate happiness depends directly upon each step taken from birth on. That potential for happiness exists in *any* normal healthy person—rich, poor or in between. Even a certain measure of success is there. But to a large extent it is *events* that will determine the actual steps taken.

In the hand we can find the inherited properties, past events that determined the steps that were taken and the success markings. We can see the future health indications (based upon inherited qualities) and *know* why the person is presently unhappy.

To achieve positive happiness (I use the term *positive* happiness because the so-called *"bliss of ignorance"* is shown by the lack of these same faculties and markings) it is a *must* that proper internal connections exist. This means logic without excessive nerves, enough energy and a receptive mind that is shown as a developed hand.

There is a difference between the developed hand and the directed hand. The *directed hand* has a direction in which it moves—usually only one or two—and is a relatively simpler hand than the undirected or mixed hand that dissipates much valuable energy on worthless or minor causes (section 109 H). The *developed hand* means only that all the faculties have been sufficiently developed, as shown by the length of the Head Line, the Thumb, and the Fingers and their length.

I will summarize the optimum markings for a hand with *potential positive happiness:*

*   An energetic, nonnervous, well-developed, directed hand.

*   A logical hand.

*   A hand without negative character markings.

Health is one of the most important factors affecting life and success. A good Life Line, a strong Head Line, good nail indications and the absence of the Health Line are good signs. But it is possible for a person to become both happy and successful even with some inherited negative health markings.

A lack of health affects the physical energy level (we are referring to an inherited general disability, not a temporary illness). It helps the person to understand the health problem when we show it as a corresponding hand-mark deformation.

Fortunately we will find offsetting positive indications in most unhealthy hands. I have found that most people with a defect also have compensating factors. (It is of interest to note that all physical or emotional inherited handicaps and their compensating factors are shown in the various lines.)

The subject's usual questions are: "Will I regain my health?" or "Will I get sick?" The answers can be based only upon the *Minor Hand* lines that show the *potential for recovery* or the *potential for disease*. We must remember that the lines in either hand may change.

If the Minor Hand shows good lines and no negative marking, there is a good chance that the Major Hand will follow suit. Unfortunately, too few observations are available to come to a correspondence principle. Especially in the area of physical and mental health, a great deal remains to be done in the way of comparing hand prints of those with similar diseases.

At present there is a growing interest on the part of hospitals and the medical profession in general, as well as by life insurance companies, in the statistical evidence hand lines may be able to give with respect to longevity and health.

It is self-evident why life insurance companies would benefit, but it is also of great benefit to people in general when the cause for abnormal hand lines will be found, and a subsequent prevention or cure made available.

Many European hospitals now routinely make hand prints of newborn infants, along with footprints, for future reference.

Homosexuality: I have studied the hands of children and young teenagers who showed homosexual tendencies, but apart from a certain greatly developed sensitivity or nervous condition, I have been unable to pinpoint definite characteristics in these hands. In the majority of adult homosexuals I see a very definite, greatly developed Girdle of Venus.

The strange thing is that this very highly developed Girdle of Venus is encountered in all types of people, as would be expected from the fact that I have seen homosexuality among all Mount types.

I cannot say that a well-developed Girdle of Venus leads to

homosexuality, but the homosexual almost invariably carries the sign. This leads me to believe that the combination leading to homosexuality consists of a developed Girdle of Venus plus other, as yet to be defined, line deviations.

Logic is implied by the second phalanx of the Thumb.

Logic guides the energy, and also accepts the possible lack thereof. Until we know much more about the body and its chemistry, it will be hard to change the drive that each of us possesses.

Love: The types of love shown in the hand fall in two categories: *simple attachments* and long-term *compound friendships* that are not divided in love for either sex.

The simple attachment and the compound friendship may both be lasting for life. It is the *level* of mentality of the subject that decides whether the love is the former or the latter.

Simple attachments are shown in the Affection Lines. They are the measure of the number of emotional involvements that have a traumatic impact. When seen in the basic hand types, they are simple attachments and no more.

Short Fingers, a short Thumb, a short and straight Head Line, undeveloped Mounts, the palm devoid of lines all denote a simple attachment, since the capacity for more than just this form of love is lacking in such a hand.

Note that very few people with this type of hand will ever ask about love: Sex is important to them, love is secondary.

The *compound friendship* is normal love of a higher order. These attachments are based, at least temporarily, upon physical and emotional compatibility. The compatibility is often a fiction, but the wish for more than the simple attachment is formulated in the subject's mind.

In the hand we find the compound friendship similarly marked in the Affection Lines, but we can see from the hand in general that we are dealing with a *second-order mentality*. The *higher-order mentality* has longer Fingers, many clearly marked lines, a developed hand and a long Thumb.

Both the normal and abnormal hand are capable of expressing compound friendships since they are both of higher-order mentality.

The compound friendship, both physical and emotional, is limited by time. We can see these limits in the Companion Lines that follow the Fate and Life Lines (sections 18 B and 32 A).

In some cases the limit is the ultimate death of one of the two partners—which is conceivably the best end for such compound friendships (section 46 deals with this matter).

The problem that is often encountered in these *higher-order attachments* is an error of judgment in one or both partners, namely *the improper interpretation of seemingly important characteristics*. This error is one of the major causes of divorce, and is avoidable if the hand lines of the partners are compared and analyzed (see *Compatibility*).

Negative markings: We have located the negative markings on the Mounts in section 120. These markings were lines weakening the qualities of the Mounts themselves. We have also shown the grille markings and cross to be similarly restrictive and negative reinforcing respectively.

Now we are concerned with the hand we examine that has negative markings of another form: The hand does not help the future development of the person, but shows a downhill progress. Where do we see this taking place?

First of all, when we compare the Minor and Major Hands we see that the Major Hand is less developed than the Minor Hand. Then we notice that the Major Hand is weak in vertical lines on the Mounts. Since these are the endings of the Fate and Sun Lines, there is no upswing in later life. When we see this lack of later-life development, note the quality of the Life Line at middle age and see if sickness is indicated.

Carefully examine the Minor Hand Life Line for event markings, which denote how much the person will be influenced by others. If the hand is a mixed one, a direction must be found in which to steer the person. Look for:

Genetic health defects: From a hand print, the hand line expert always knows that a person is unhealthy, just as the medical profession sees it upon studying the actual physical body.

Weak lines indicate *weak people:* People with weak hand lines should follow a way of life that will not tax them overly much. The hand with weak lines is more susceptible to minor illnesses—of which the subject often has many. But he can live to an old age. It is especially important to recognize the weak lines in the small child so that there will not be an excessive physical burden placed upon him. At present it is not possible to strengthen weak lines in a hand; exercise does not improve them.

Genetic emotional defects are found in the Head Line and the lines on the Mount of Luna.

This is the area where topographical palmistry can be very helpful. The defects are quite obvious upon examining the hand print and are available for inspection at a very early age. They are carried in the Head Line, both Minor and Major Hands and in the area of Luna.

It is possible to predict when an emotional defect will become a damaging factor. It is carried in the *Head Line code and dated*.

The analyst must be very careful not to unduly worry the person who is being examined, since it is recognizing the threat that makes correction possible. The proper analysis based upon prior experience with similar cases will lead to avoiding the problem.

If the threat seems imminent, these people must be referred for proper psychiatric treatment. Palmistry can only recognize, not cure!

The first two of these negative markings, the health and emotional defects, can be successfully improved in the hand. The third—event markings found in the Life, Fate and Sun Lines —lies beyond our present knowledge.

If such a threat appears in the far future, then the analyst

[196]

should look for *positive markings*. These are the goals to which to point the subject's mind.

Such positive markings are discussed under the heading *abnormal mentality,* to which we should add that the surrounding in which these emotionally threatened people live must be sympathetic to them. So should their circle of friends and acquaintances if they are to remain stable.

Apart from telling the subject the potential outlook for health, both emotional and physical, it is also possible to project the general trend of capability and achievement.

Occupations: One of the uses to which we may put the result of our character analysis is in assessing the type of career a subject may follow with maximum chance for success.

After the character markings have been analyzed as outlined in the introductory paragraphs of Part Two, there remains the problem of matching these with presently existing careers. There is also a demand factor that requires the help of a counselor to channel the energies and personality to a trade or vocation for which there is a need.

I consider the analysis from two points of view: One helps me to place the person in a compatible surrounding, that is, compatible with his makeup; the other helps me find maximum use for his energy and knowledge so that the person will not become bored later in life.

A professional guidance counselor, with the information about the subject at hand, will be able to secure optimum placement.

Success is something that can be measured in the lines of the hand. It is revealed in the Fate Line, Sun Line and the markings on the Mounts.

The question "If no lines in my hand would change from this point on, will I become successful?" is easier to answer than the much more involved "Will I be happy?" A successful person may not be a happy person, and vice versa. To measure *happiness* in the hand requires that one consider a great many factors.

[197]

Consider: Will this person become happy with success? Does the person want fame or money? Or both? Does the hand favor the mental world or the physical? Is it basic or complex?

It is all in the values that are looked for. I must assume that *anyone* who reads this book is to a certain extent interested in two things: the *potential for achieving* and the *ultimate happiness* derived from such achievement.

Wisdom is not shown in the hand. Rather, it is the *wish* for learning, the *wish* for knowledge that is shown in the *active directed hand with good Head Lines.* Neither is ignorance shown as such: The lazy mind shows up in the elementary hand with few lines, a short Head Line and a small Thumb.

In my analysis of hands of many well-known people, I have found that the hands do not generally indicate the specific talent we ascribe to the subjects. Since my work brings me in contact with the most famous artists and performers, I would have expected to encounter a great similarity in their hands. This is not so. The only factor most great actors and directors have in common is a well-developed imagination, usually coupled with a well-developed first phalanx of the Thumb.

I have met with this same combination in the hand of very successful businessmen, so that this combination alone seems to point to success in general. It is not necessarily a form of permanent success, however; only those hands that have well-formed and long Fate or Sun Lines were traditionally considered "fortunate" hands. The reason performers are considered more "successful" than the scientist who achieves his goal, for instance, is that the performers' total goal is public recognition. They have a much simpler idea of success than most people. This very simplicity is visible in the hand print; but so is the failing. And only the permanent success is shown in the long Fate and Sun Lines.

To enable the student to analyze hand prints, I present a number that show certain peculiarities, listed as examples 1 through 6.

Part 4

Sample Readings

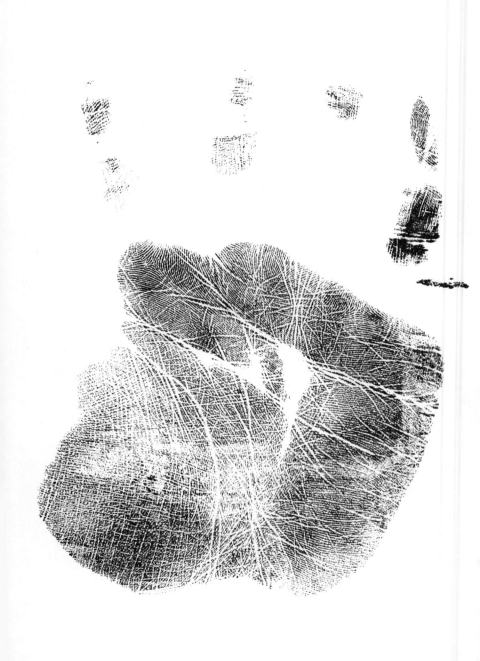

Example 1 (the print of the Major Hand of the subject)

Life Line. The Life Line runs normally, although rather close to the Thumb, narrowing the Venus area. This gives a rather cold personality. There are no heavy event lines crossing the Life Line, with one exception, although there are minor crossing lines at ages 11, 17, 19, 22, 25 and into the 30's. They tend to disappear with advancing age. This indicates a nervous condition that disappears in later life. There are events connected with the crossing lines, but they are mostly generated by the emotions. One exception is an event line from Venus at age 18 cutting the Life Line, the Head Line and vaguely ending in the area of Mars, under Saturn. This line may be the indication of a severe head injury which this young man suffered at about that age. Note that the Fate Line ends at the Head Line in the left hand. The lines that drop down from the Life Line in the early age period are the starting points of Influence Lines showing the family relationship of the subject. One conspicuous Influence Line starts at age 18, continues to age 26 and then merges again with the Life Line, which determines the end of a relationship or friendship. Another such line, starting at about age 12, veers further from the Life Line into the Venus area and then rejoins the Life Line at about age 32. Such a line means that the influence of a person is felt strongly at the beginning and ending of that line; in the intermediate period this person was influencing the subject rather remotely. The fact that the influence stops suddenly at age 32 often is an indication that the influential person has died or moved far away from the subject.

The side of the Life Line located away from the Thumb shows two other types of lines besides the event lines discussed earlier. One is a series of Success Lines appearing at regular and short intervals all along the first thirty or thirty-five years of life. They are minor achievements and quite intensive during that period, showing great activity. Notice, however, that almost without exception there are downward, negative lines connected with every one of them. The successes and failures are constantly interconnected. The sum total for this type Life Line spells hectic activity.

The health indicated on the Life Line is excellent, so that the activity will not be detrimental to the subject. The travel line is almost hidden by the other lines descending from the Life Line, but with a little care it can easily be detected at about age 40 (somewhat high on the Life Line) descending as a strong line and dropping into the Fate Line. There are lines branching off from the Fate Line at about the same period, but these lines do not join the Life Line, they only ascend toward it.

The *Head Line* follows a normal course but shows a large number of crosslines at the beginning, indicating again a great variety of interests. The Head Line straightens out a great deal in later life. The most remarkable point concerning the Head Line is the starting position: The excessive distance between the Life Line and the Head Line at the start denotes excessive independence to the point of foolhardiness.

Lack of judgment accounts for the many little Success and Failure Lines on the Life Line. The popular way to describe this person would be to consider him unrealistic but very energetic. Note that the Head Line shows branching to Luna and a fork: The mind is potentially brilliant and imaginative, it is just the judgment that is lacking.

The Heart Line is considered in two ways: as describing the physical organ and also describing the emotions. My considerations involve the physical organ more than the emotions, since I have already determined from the Life Line where the major influences stop and start. For the deeper emotions I look at the Marriage Lines. (For the interpretation of the Heart Line as expressing the emotional life of the subject, see section 26 A and B.) The physical organ is shown in this hand print to be average in makeup. The tasseling at the end of the Heart Line is common in most hands, and the only slight variation noticed is that there is some evidence of layering (more than one line running parallel) under the Ring Finger. This may mean an emotional rather than a physical disturbance at the age indicated.

The Fate Line also shows the general nature of the subject. It starts many times and veers continually toward the area of Venus. Especially between the ages of 5(!) and 25 are there many of these new starts. The end of the Fate Line is weak under Saturn but is replaced by a grouping of lines under Apollo: It spells success, but no money or power over others.

The Health Line is absent, which reinforces the good health indicated by the Life Line quality.

The Marriage Line or Affection Lines in this print have been obtained by rolling the hand off toward the percussion, which artificially widens the lines on the side of the hand. The very end of these lines is found around the side of the hand, which would not normally show on a hand print. There are two distinctly marked affection lines: one at about age 27, the other high up in the age level—perhaps 35 or older. A slight line crosses the first (lower) of these Affection Lines, which according to early palmists spelled a bad ending for the relationship. Due to a lack of specialized research in recent times, the interpretation of this line is still cloudy, although it seems definitely to be a line dealing with the emotional life rather than events.

The Jupiter area in this particular hand is calm, without either vertical or horizontal major lines. The very minor blocking lines need no attention since they appear in the "quiet" part of the palm. Saturn is lacking in vertical development, indicating the lack of financial success or power over others in later life. But there is no blocking condition either; there is no lack of success, though obviously the success is not determined by money or power. The development under Apollo shows us why the Saturn underdevelopment is unimportant: Success is visible in the personal achievement of the subject, in a multiple art career. Great success in the arts is not indicated—there are far too many Success Lines—and there is some blocking by horizontal lines. If extreme success were indicated, the hand would show a Money Line in the form of a vertical, unblocked line on Saturn.

A rather surprising development is the low activity on Mercury. Frantic physical activity is shown as vertical lines on Mercury. Athletes and great businessmen have highly-developed Mercury markings. This hand shows that there is no great physical exertion; the frenzied activity is mental. The areas of Mars are quiet, denoting a basically peace-loving person who will not intentionally attack or get involved in arguments not directly concerning him. The area of Venus also shows a rather good disposition, although not overly warm or involved with the opposite sex. A somewhat more complete development in the area of Luna shows many Travel Lines and a great wish for constant change, which may be the underlying key to the entire personality.

I had the pleasure of examining the hands of a gentleman in his early 50's who asked me to analyze his hands as to his future possibilities. Upon examining his Major Hand, I noticed a very pronounced island in the Life Line starting at the age of about 40 and disappearing again at age 47 or 48. I immediately mentioned that he had been ill for a number of years, but that this illness was to disappear at this time. I mentioned the type of illness, which was shown as a disturbance of the Head Line, and indicated a mental condition.

After identifying a number of event lines crossing the Life Line at various ages, he asked me if I could see something special about his early life. I noticed only that there was a conflict in the family for religious reasons. He then asked me if it was not possible for me to see that he was one of twins. I was not able to see that, but I then asked him if his identical twin brother had also suffered from the same mental disturbance. He replied no. I examined the Minor Hand then—in which there was no island in the Life Line. "I will give you odds," I said to him, "that your brother has the same hands as you have, but that he is left-handed and his right hand corresponds to your left hand." He then said with surprise that his identical twin brother was indeed left-handed.

I examined the hands of a well-known actress of British extraction who asked me what the dominant tendency in her hand was. I was to get a very great surprise, for instead of finding a very extroverted artistic hand, I discovered that the entire hand pointed sharply to the imagination. She had a well-developed Mount of Luna, with a very sloping Head Line, all of which showed the imagination well developed. The Sun Line was almost entirely missing, and the entire hand followed closely the development of the Major Hand of Sir Arthur Sullivan. (This should remind us of the fact that we cannot see the gender from a palm print.) I could not hide my surprise to see this development in the hands of such a well-known star. She smiled at me and said, "You may not realize that my greatest interest, and one which I will ultimately want to follow, is to be a writer, not an actress."

It is conceivable, therefore, that one's taken profession will not show in the hand as clearly as the *actual* greatest talent and desire. A talented writer may very often have all the attributes to be a fine performer, due to the extreme development of the imagination, but not many performers may have the imagination needed to be great writers.

Examining the hands of one of our most famous dancing, acting directors, one who has been foremost in show business for a great many years, I noticed that everything in his hands pointed to the Little Fingers. They seemed bent toward a point between Apollo and Mercury. The subject also displayed very developed Sun and Mercury Lines.

Developed Mercury denotes an athlete and a businessman; developed Apollo, the artist. When I see a print of a hand with a great deal of Mercury development as well as Apollo, there are only a few combinations possible. We are dealing with a great businessman who collects art; an artist with a great sense of business; a top athlete who is an art connoisseur and collector; or we are dealing with an athletic artist— the dancer. Note that this hand represented all these qualities, and more.

I do not know of any combination of Mercury and Apollo that is negative. Mercury alone can make a crook, but the combination with Apollo, denoting the love of art, does not make this a thief of art treasures for the sake of art. Possibly for the sake of money, but then there will not be a so-called Sun Line and developed Apollo.

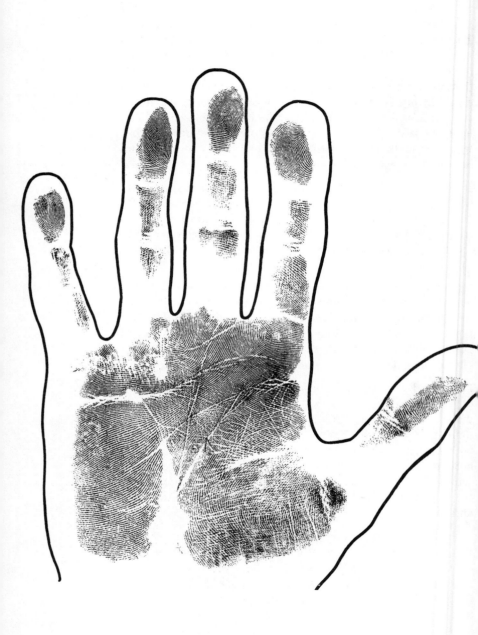

Example 2

The most outstanding event line in this example is a line at 24 to 25 years of age, crossing the Fate Line and going into and stopping at the Heart Line. This is a typical example of section 12 C. The actual event was the subject's father getting killed in an airplane crash at that age. As a matter of interest, the line was not easily found when I gave the hand a visual examination, but it stands out quite clearly in the print. (Holding hands may be pleasurable in some instances, but it is not conducive to excellence in palmistry.) The early Life Line shows illnesses, and a long bout with pneumonia is shown at about 6 to 7 years of age. Note the chained pattern at early age. Part of the Girdle of Venus is visible, which together with the sloping Head Line gives us the sensitivity and imagination this gentleman requires as a writer. The Fate Line doubles after reaching the Head Line and indicates the doubling of careers in two stages between ages 35 and 50. The little downward lines from the Heart Line show small disappointments where the relationship with other people is concerned. One very nice sign in this hand is the continuation of the Fate Line to well under the Middle Finger, although with small interruptions (which I can easily detect in the print but which were not to be seen easily from the hand itself). When I was checking event lines—I found one small puzzling line in this hand—namely the line seemingly originating in the Life Line, age 13 to 14, cutting the Head Line, and terminating before touching the Fate Line. When looking very closely with a magnifying glass, I can imagine that this is an event line starting in the area of Venus, but it is very ill-defined. The subject does not remember any event corresponding to this line.

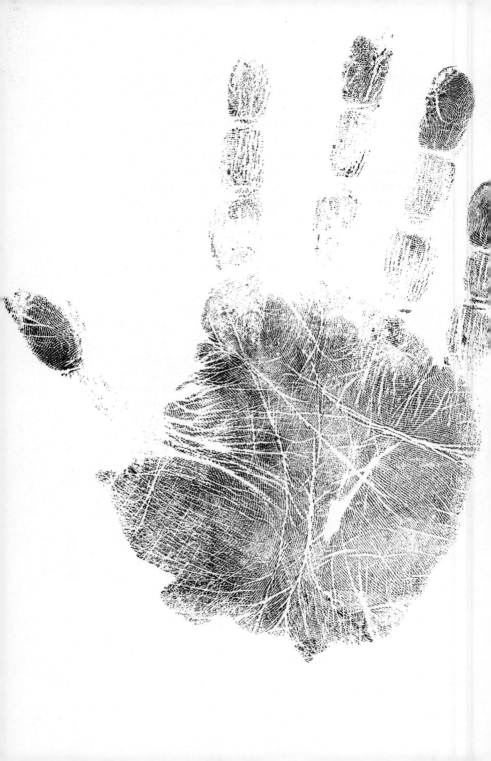

Example 3

This is a fine example of an emotionally very busy hand. The lines are too clearly defined to be considered nervous: We are dealing with a very complex hand. The first event line determination is the 11-year marking that touches the Head Line. At that point it sends offshoots up to the Middle Finger, sends a branch to the Fate Line and continues to the Heart Line. Some great emotional upheaval shows itself in this manner. At 17 or 18 years of age another very strong event line crosses the Head Line and the Fate Line and runs into the Heart Line, showing a grave shock to the affections. A small even line appears a year or so later, and at about 19 another complete destructive event line runs with a curve into the Mount of Apollo. Note again that at the point where this line crosses and cuts the Head Line, a branch is sent out into the area of Mars. Emotional upheaval is well hidden by the Head Line, running straight to the area of the imagination. Large numbers of Travel Lines indicate the wish for change. This hand shows great activity in the imagination at a later age. The only things that stand between this example and the hand of a prophet are the lack of an Intuition Line and the poorly marked Health Line, which saps this hand of the necessary strength in its early years. Also the Fate Line is overshadowed by the multiplicity of the Apollo or Sun Lines.

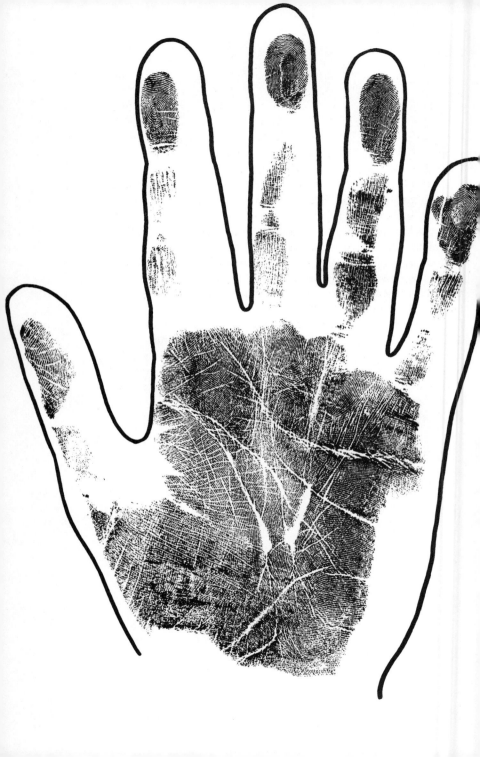

Example 4

This hand print is given as an example of the doubling of the Head Line, not a very common occurrence. One Head Line follows a rather twisting path toward Luna, and a second Head Line seemingly comes down from Saturn and sweeps down toward Mars-Mercury.

This kind of development is found in many people who have suffered great emotional upheaval. The basic Head Line is the normal pattern: in this case, of an accomplished writer with great imagination. The subject became a political refugee at an early age and suffered greatly. The line connecting the two Head Line sections so conspicuously at age 17 to 20 (read on the Life Line) marks the period of emotional changeover. The Fate and Sun Lines both show development after maturity. Jupiter shows slight blocking and Saturn, Apollo and Mercury minor development, although the Sun Line is rather clearly marked in the later age period, where it spells a certain amount of success—probably literary in nature due to the original slope of the Head Line.

The very strong line from the wrist to Luna may be the start of the Fate Line, which veers sharply at age 8 or 9, indicating complete physical change of residence and living.

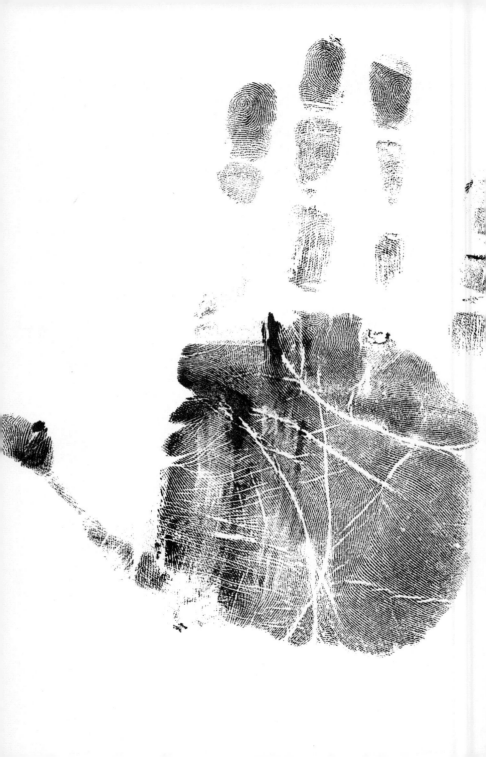

Example 5

This hand is a simple one; the lines are few and clearly shown. The Life Line shows a small irregularity at 20 to 21 years of age, usually indicating a change of surrounding. The change is concurrent with a small Success Line ascending from the Life Line at that period, another indication of the same change. There are event lines at age 18 and 25, but neither crosses the Life Line and thus they do not influence the subject. Another small change line is shown at about age 50, again accompanied by a small Success Line. The Fate Line is straight up to age 47 or 48 and then continues, with a small interruption, to an advanced age. After 47 or 48 years, the doubling of the Fate Line shows duplicity of careers. Success comes late in life, and not too strongly indicated by the Sun Line. The line of Mercury or Health Line shows a good capability in commerce and athletics; the Heart Line is simple, like the other lines, and unemotional. The Head Line is straight and average, not showing unusual imagination, nor a lack of intelligence. The Travel Lines on Luna are developed more than would be expected from this hand—an outstanding feature giving a restless nature.

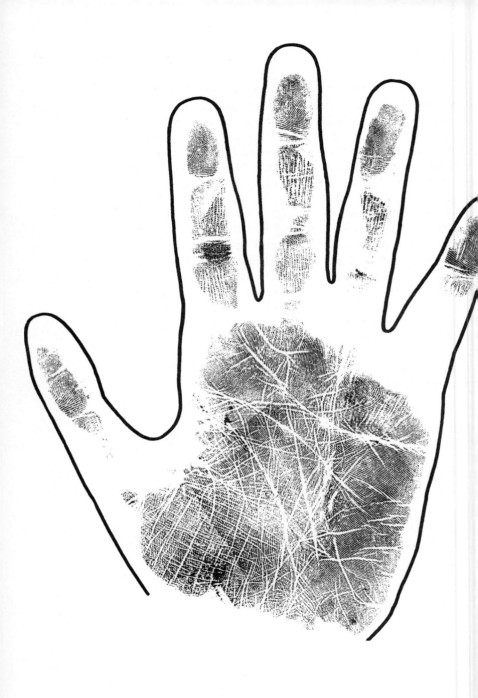

Example 6

This is a very difficult hand to analyze. The Life Line and in fact all lines in the hand show some form of doubling. It is hard to select characteristic lines because the multiplicity of detail hides them.

At about 5 years of age, a line from the Life Line runs through the Head Line into the Heart Line. At about 8 years of age a Trauma Line crosses the Life Line. At age 8 to 9, a Trauma Line from the Life Line runs to the Fate Line. Between 25 and 35 years, a group of Achievement Lines ascend from the Life Line. Doubled Fate Lines and multiple Sun Lines date from early childhood. There is blocking of Jupiter and heavy blocking of Saturn, blocking of Apollo and activity on Mercury, showing a good mind. Great activity in the travel areas of Luna and generally a very active hand. This would be a very successful hand but for the Ring of Saturn being so heavily marked.

There are two outstanding event lines, one at about age 8, if read on the Life Line, or age 10 when read on the Head Line crossing, even up to age 12. To check, see if this was a very independent child.

The second event line at about age 16 is a Trauma Line, showing that a very disturbing event took place. It reads like the violent death of a close friend or relative. The maximum age is 18 years old. In any case, it is an accidental death, no sickness on the part of the person who was lost.

There is a complete change of surroundings at age 9 due to an occurrence in the family. Shortly after age 9 or 10 this person lived with other people till the dramatic event at age 17 or 18 (see above).

The Trauma Line at 7 or 8 years of age is also a family loss, similar to the 18-year one but from an illness, probably heart disease.